MORE
Windows® 98
Simplified™

IDG's 3-D Visual™ Series

IDG BOOKS *From* **maranGraphics™**

IDG Books Worldwide, Inc.
An International Data Group Company
Foster City, CA • Indianapolis • Chicago • New York

More Windows® 98 Simplified™

Published by
IDG Books Worldwide, Inc.
An International Data Group Company
919 E. Hillsdale Blvd., Suite 400
Foster City, CA 94404
(650) 655-3000

Library of Congress Catalog Card No.: 98-075156

ISBN: 0-7645-6037-9

Printed in the United States of America
10 9 8 7 6 5 4 3 2 1

Distributed in the United States by IDG Books Worldwide, Inc.

Distributed by Transworld Publishers Limited in the United Kingdom; by IDG Norge Books for Norway; by IDG Sweden Books for Sweden; by Woodslane Pty. Ltd. for Australia; by Woodslane (NZ) Ltd. for New Zealand; by Addison Wesley Longman Singapore Pte Ltd. for Singapore, Malaysia, Thailand, Indonesia and Korea; by Norma Comunicaciones S.A. for Colombia; by Intersoft for South Africa; by International Thomson Publishing for Germany, Austria and Switzerland; by Toppan Company Ltd. for Japan; by Distribuidora Cuspide for Argentina; by Livraria Cultura for Brazil; by Ediciencia S.A. for Ecuador; by Ediciones ZETA S.C.R. Ltda. for Peru; by WS Computer Publishing Corporation, Inc., for the Philippines; by Unalis Corporation for Taiwan; by Contemporanea de Ediciones for Venezuela; by Computer Book & Magazine Store for Puerto Rico; by Express Computer Distributors for the Caribbean and West Indies. Authorized Sales Agent: Anthony Rudkin Associates for the Middle East and North Africa.
For corporate orders, please call maranGraphics at 800-469-6616.
For general information on IDG Books Worldwide's books in the U.S., please call our Consumer Customer Service department at 800-762-2974.
For reseller information, including discounts and premium sales, please call our Reseller Customer Service department at 800-434-3422.
For information on where to purchase IDG Books Worldwide's books outside the U.S., please contact our International Sales department at 650-655-3200 or fax 650-655-3297.
For information on foreign language translations, please contact our Foreign & Subsidiary Rights department at 650-655-3021 or fax 650-655-3281.
For sales inquiries and special prices for bulk quantities, please contact our Sales department at 650-655-3200.
For information on using IDG Books Worldwide's books in the classroom or for ordering examination copies, please contact our Educational Sales department at 800-434-2086 or fax 317-596-5499.
For press review copies, author interviews, or other publicity information, please contact our Public Relations department at 650-655-3000 or fax 650-655-3299.
For authorization to photocopy items for corporate, personal, or educational use, please contact maranGraphics at 800-469-6616.

Trademark Acknowledgments

Permissions

The 3-D illustrations are the copyright of maranGraphics, Inc.

U.S. Corporate Sales	U.S. Trade Sales
Contact maranGraphics at (800) 469-6616 or Fax (905) 890-9434.	Contact IDG Books at (800) 434-3422 or (650) 655-3000.

Welcome to the world of IDG Books Worldwide.

IDG Books Worldwide, Inc., is a subsidiary of International Data Group, the world's largest publisher of computer-related information and the leading global provider of information services on information technology. IDG was founded more than 25 years ago and now employs more than 8,500 people worldwide. IDG publishes more than 270 computer publications in over 75 countries (see listing below). More than 90 million people read one or more IDG publications each month.

Launched in 1990, IDG Books Worldwide is today the #1 publisher of best-selling computer books in the United States. We are proud to have received eight awards from the Computer Press Association in recognition of editorial excellence and three from Computer Currents' First Annual Readers' Choice Awards. Our best-selling ...For Dummies® series has more than 25 million copies in print with translations in 30 languages. IDG Books Worldwide, through a joint venture with IDG's Hi-Tech Beijing, became the first U.S. publisher to publish a computer book in the People's Republic of China. In record time, IDG Books Worldwide has become the first choice for millions of readers around the world who want to learn how to better manage their businesses.

Our mission is simple: Every one of our books is designed to bring extra value and skill-building instructions to the reader. Our books are written by experts who understand and care about our readers. The knowledge base of our editorial staff comes from years of experience in publishing, education, and journalism - experience which we use to produce books for the '90s. In short, we care about books, so we attract the best people. We devote special attention to details such as audience, interior design, use of icons, and illustrations. And because we use an efficient process of authoring, editing, and desktop publishing our books electronically, we can spend more time ensuring superior content and spend less time on the technicalities of making books.

You can count on our commitment to deliver high-quality books at competitive prices on topics you want to read about. At IDG Books Worldwide, we continue in the IDG tradition of delivering quality for more than 25 years. You'll find no better book on a subject than one from IDG Books Worldwide.

John Kilcullen   Steven Berkowitz
CEO   President and Publisher
IDG Books Worldwide, Inc.   IDG Books Worldwide, Inc.

IDG Books Worldwide, Inc., is a subsidiary of International Data Group, the world's largest publisher of computer-related information and the leading global provider of information services on information technology. International Data Group publishes over 276 computer publications in over 75 countries. Ninety million people read one or more International Data Group publications each month. International Data Group's publications include: Argentina: Annuario de Informatica, Computerworld Argentina, PC World Argentina; Australia: Australian Macworld, Client/Server Journal, Computer Living, Computerworld, Computerworld 100, Digital News, IT Casebook, Network World, On-line World Australia, PC World, Publishing Essentials, Reseller, WebMaster; Austria: Computerwelt Osterreich, Networks Austria, PC Tip; Belarus: PC World Belarus; Belgium: Data News; Brazil: Annuário de Informática, Computerworld Brazil, Connections, Super Game Power, Macworld, PC Player, PC World Brazil, Publish Brazil, Reseller News; Bulgaria: Computerworld Bulgaria, Networkworld/Bulgaria, PC & MacWorld Bulgaria; Canada: CIO Canada, Client/Server World, ComputerWorld Canada, InfoCanada, Network World Canada; Chile: Computerworld Chile, PC World Chile; Colombia: Computerworld Colombia, PC World Colombia; Costa Rica: PC World Centro America; The Czech and Slovak Republics: Computerworld Czechoslovakia, Elektronika Czechoslovakia, Macworld Czech Republic, PC World Czechoslovakia; Denmark: Communications World, Computerworld Danmark, Macworld Danmark, PC Privat Danmark, PC World Danmark, PC World Danmark Supplements, TECH World; Dominican Republic: PC World Republica Dominicana; Ecuador: PC World Ecuador; Egypt: Computerworld Middle East, PC World Middle East; El Salvador: PC World Centro America; Finland: MikroPC, Tietoverkko, Tietoviikko; France: Distributique, Golden, Hebdo-Distributique, Info PC, Le Guide du Monde Informatique, Le Monde Informatique, Reseaux & Telecoms; Germany: Computer Partner, Computerwoche, Computerwoche Extra, Computerwoche Focus, I/M Information Management, Macwelt, PC Welt; Greece: GamePro, Multimedia World; Guatemala: PC World Centro America; Honduras: PC World Centro America; Hong Kong: Computerworld Hong Kong, PCWorld Hong Kong, Publish in Asia; Hungary: ABCD CD-ROM, Computerworld Szamitastechnika, PC & Mac World Hungary, PC-X Magazine; Iceland: Tolvuheimur/PC World Island; India: Information Systems Computerworld, PC World India, Publish in Asia; Indonesia: InfoKomputer PC World, Komputek Computerworld, Publish in Asia; Ireland: ComputerScope, PC Live!; Israel: People & Computers; Italy: Computerworld Italia, Computerworld Italia Special Editions, Macworld Italia, Networking Italia, PC Shopping, PC World Italia, PC World/Walt Disney; Japan: DTP World, HP Open World Japan, Macworld Japan, Nikkei Personal Computing, Open World Japan, OS/2 World Japan, SunWorld Japan, Windows World Japan; Kenya: East African Computer News; Korea: Hi-Tech Information/Computerworld, Macworld Korea, PC World Korea; Macedonia: PC World Macedonia; Malaysia: Computerworld Malaysia, PC World Malaysia, Publish in Asia; Mexico: Computerworld Mexico, Macworld, PC World Mexico; Myanmar: PC World Myanmar; Netherlands: Computer! Totaal, LAN Magazine, LanWorld Buyers Guide, Macworld, Net Magazine, Totaal! Beurskrant; New Zealand: Absolute Beginner's Guide, Computer Buyer, Computer Industry Directory, Computerworld New Zealand, MTB, Network World, PC World New Zealand; Nicaragua: PC World Centro America; Nigeria: PC World Nigeria; Norway: Computerworld Norge, Computerworld Privat (Datamagasinet), CW Rapport Norge, IDG's KURSGUIDE, Macworld Norge, Multimediaworld, PC World Ekspress, PC World Nettverk, PC World Norge, PC World's Produktguide, Windows World Spesial; Pakistan: Computerworld Pakistan, PC World Pakistan; Panama: PC World Panama; P. R. of China: China Computer Users, China Computerworld, China Infoworld, China Telecom World Weekly, Computer & Communication, Electronic Design China, Electronics Today, Electronics Weekly, Game Camp, Game Soft, Network World China, PC World China, Popular Computer Weekly, Software Weekly, Software World, Telecom World; Peru: Computerworld Peru, PC World Profesional Peru, PC World Peru; Poland: Computerworld Poland, Computerworld Special Report, Macworld, Networld, PC World Komputer, Philippines: Computerworld Philippines, PC World Philippines, Publish in Asia; Portugal: Cerebro/PC World, Computerworld/Correio Informático, Dealer World Portugal, Mac*In/PC*In, Multimedia World Portugal; Puerto Rico: PC World Puerto Rico; Romania: Computerworld Romania, PC World Romania, Telecom Romania; Russia: Computerworld Russia, Mir PK, Sety; Singapore: Computerworld Singapore, PC World Singapore, Publish in Asia; Slovenia: MONITOR; South Africa: Computing S.A., InfoWorld S.A., Network World S.A., Software World; Spain: Computerworld Espa-a, COMUNICACIONES WORLD, Dealer World, Macworld Espa-a, PC World Espa-a; Sweden: CAP&Design, Computer Sweden, Corporate Computing, MacWorld, Maxi Data, MikroDatorn, Natverk & Kommunikation, PC/Aktiv, PC World, Windows World; Switzerland: Computerworld Schweiz, Macworld Schweiz, PCtip; Taiwan: Computerworld Taiwan, Macworld Taiwan, PC World Taiwan, Publish Taiwan, Windows World; Thailand: Thai Computerworld, Publish in Asia; Turkey: Computerworld Turkiye, MACWORLD Turkiye, PC WORLD Turkiye; Ukraine: Computerworld Kiev, Computers & Software, Multimedia World Ukraine, PC World Ukraine; United Kingdom: Acorn User, Amiga Action, Amiga Computing, Appletalk, Computing, GamePro, Macworld, Network News, Parents and Computers, PC Advisor, PC Home, PSX Pro UK, The WEB; United States: Cable in the Classroom, CD Review, CIO Magazine, Computerworld, Computerworld Client/Server Journal, Digital Video Magazine, DOS World, Federal Computer Week, GamePro, InfoWorld, I-Way, JavaWorld, Macworld, Multimedia World, Netscape World Online, Network World, PC Entertainment, PC World, Publish, SunWorld Online, SWATPro Magazine, Video Event, WebMaster; Uruguay: PC World Uruguay; Venezuela: Computerworld Venezuela, PC World Venezuela; and Vietnam: PC World Vietnam.

**Every maranGraphics book represents
the extraordinary vision and commitment of a unique family:
the Maran family of Toronto, Canada.**

Back Row (from left to right): *Sherry Maran, Rob Maran, Richard Maran, Maxine Maran, Jill Maran.*
Front Row (from left to right): *Judy Maran, Ruth Maran.*

Richard Maran is the company founder and its inspirational leader. He developed maranGraphics' proprietary communication technology called "visual grammar." This book is built on that technology—empowering readers with the easiest and quickest way to learn about computers.

Ruth Maran is the Author and Architect—a role Richard established that now bears Ruth's distinctive touch. She creates the words and visual structure that are the basis for the books.

Judy Maran is the Project Manager. She works with Ruth, Richard and the highly talented maranGraphics illustrators, designers and editors to transform Ruth's material into its final form.

Rob Maran is the Technical and Production Specialist. He makes sure the state-of-the-art technology used to create these books always performs as it should.

Sherry Maran manages the Reception, Order Desk and any number of areas that require immediate attention and a helping hand.

Jill Maran is a jack-of-all-trades who works in the Accounting and Human Resources department.

Maxine Maran is the Business Manager and family sage. She maintains order in the business and family—and keeps everything running smoothly.

Oh, and three other family members are seated on the sofa. These graphic disk characters help make it fun and easy to learn about computers. They're part of the extended maranGraphics family.

Credits

Author & Architect:
Ruth Maran

Copy Development Director:
Kelleigh Wing

Copy Development:
Roxanne Van Damme
Cathy Benn

Project Manager:
Judy Maran

Editing & Screen Captures:
Raquel Scott
Jason M. Brown
Janice Boyer
Michelle Kirchner
James Menzies
Frances Lea
Emmet Mellow

Layout Designer:
Treena Lees

Illustrators:
Russ Marini
Jamie Bell
Peter Grecco

Illustrators & Screen Artists:
Jeff Jones
Sean Johannesen
Steven Schaerer

Indexer:
Raquel Scott

Permissions Coordinator:
Jenn Hillman

Post Production:
Robert Maran

Editorial Support:
Michael Roney

Acknowledgments

Thanks to the dedicated staff of maranGraphics, including
Jamie Bell, Cathy Benn, Janice Boyer, Jason M. Brown,
Francisco Ferreira, Peter Grecco, Jenn Hillman, Sean Johannesen,
Jeff Jones, Michelle Kirchner, Wanda Lawrie, Frances Lea,
Treena Lees, Jill Maran, Judy Maran, Maxine Maran,
Robert Maran, Sherry Maran, Russ Marini, Emmet Mellow,
James Menzies, Steven Schaerer, Raquel Scott,
Roxanne Van Damme, Paul Whitehead and Kelleigh Wing.

Finally, to Richard Maran who originated the easy-to-use
graphic format of this guide. Thank you for your
inspiration and guidance.

Table of Contents

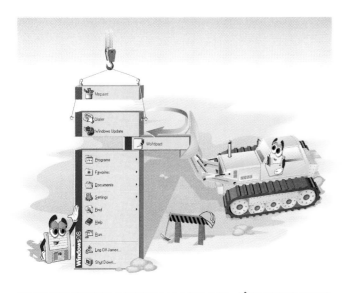

CHAPTER 4

CUSTOMIZE WINDOWS

CHAPTER 5

OPTIMIZE YOUR COMPUTER

CHAPTER 6

BACK UP FILES

Table of Contents

CHAPTER 7

WORK ON A NETWORK

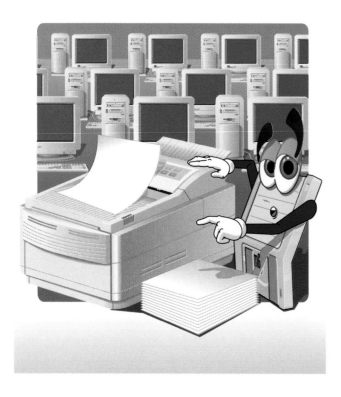

CHAPTER 8

EXCHANGE E-MAIL

CHAPTER *11*

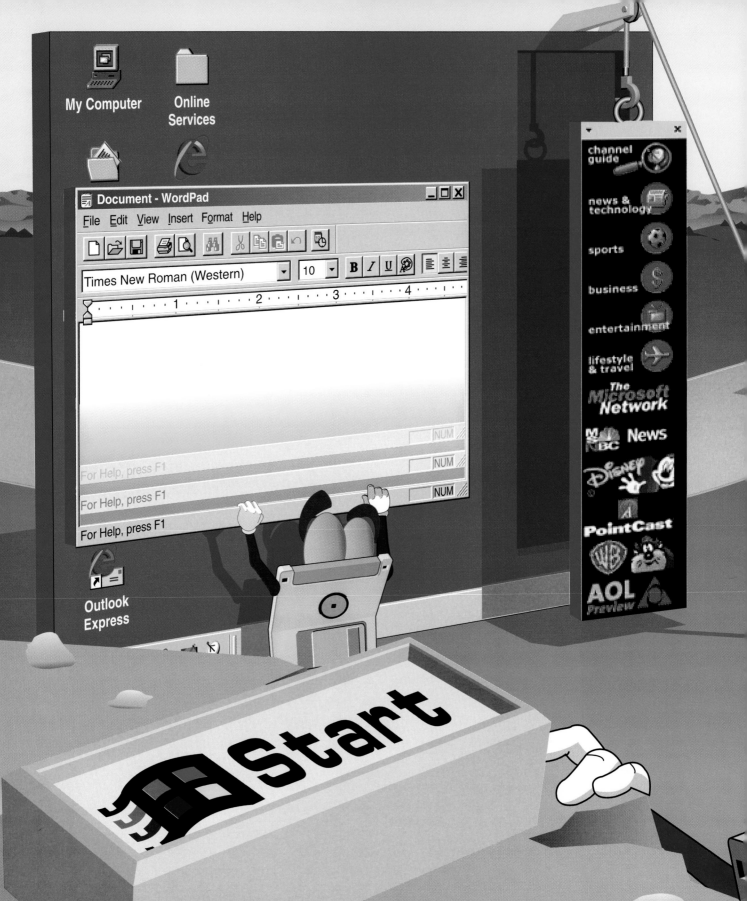

CHAPTER 1

REVIEW OF WINDOWS BASICS

Do you need to review the basic skills required to work with Windows 98? This chapter shows you how to start a program, move and size a window, show the desktop and more.

Microsoft® Windows® 98 is a program that controls the overall activity of your computer.

Windows ensures that all parts of your computer work together smoothly and efficiently.

Work With Files and Programs

Windows helps you work with the files stored on your computer. You can display file properties, show hidden files and back up files. Windows also allows you to create documents, record sounds and make telephone calls from your computer.

Customize and Optimize Your Computer

Windows allows you to customize and optimize your computer. You can rearrange the items on the Start menu, use accessibility features, change the power management settings and install new programs.

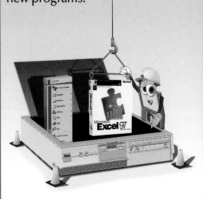

Exchange Information

You can use Windows to exchange electronic mail, participate in newsgroups, communicate with others over the Internet and create your own Web pages.

The Windows 98 screen consists of various items. The items that appear depend on the setup of your computer.

My Computer

Lets you view all the folders and files stored on your computer.

My Documents

Provides a convenient place to store your documents.

Network Neighborhood

Lets you view all the folders and files available on your network.

Recycle Bin

Stores deleted files and allows you to recover them later.

Title Bar

Displays the name of an open window.

Window

A rectangle on your screen that displays information.

Desktop

The background area of your screen.

Start Button

Gives you quick access to programs, files and Windows Help.

Quick Launch Toolbar

Gives you quick access to commonly used features, including Internet Explorer, Outlook Express, the desktop and channels.

Taskbar

Displays a button for each open window on your screen. You can use these buttons to switch between open windows.

Channel Bar

Displays specially designed Web sites you can have Windows automatically deliver to your computer.

Windows provides an easy, graphical way for you to use your computer. Windows automatically starts when you turn on your computer.

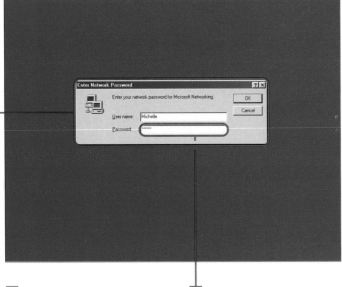

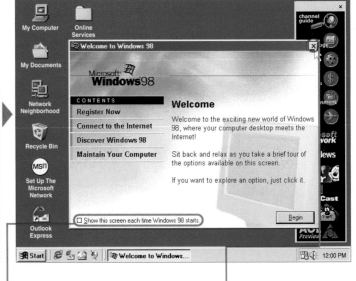

1 Turn on your computer and monitor.

■ A dialog box may appear, asking you to enter your password.

2 Type your password and then press the **Enter** key.

■ The Welcome to Windows 98 dialog box appears.

3 If you do not want this dialog box to appear each time you start Windows, move the mouse ⌖ over this option and then press the left button (☑ changes to ☐).

4 To close the dialog box, move the mouse ⌖ over ☒ and then press the left button.

What is the Channel Bar?

The Channel Bar displays
specially designed Web sites
that Windows can automatically
deliver to your computer. When
you first start Windows, the
Channel Bar appears on your
desktop. You can remove the
Channel Bar if you want to free
up space on your desktop.

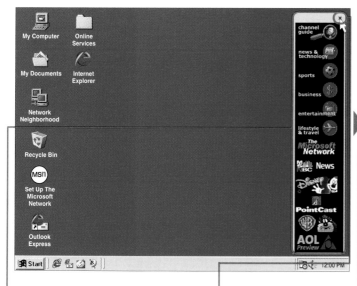

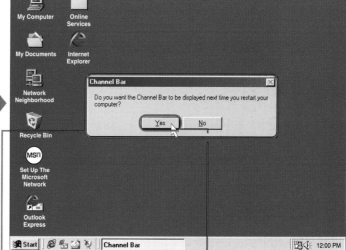

REMOVE THE CHANNEL BAR

■ When you first start
Windows, the Channel Bar
appears on your desktop.

1 To remove the Channel
Bar, position the mouse ⌖
over the top edge of the
Channel Bar. A gray bar
appears.

2 Move the mouse ⌖
over **X** and then press
the left button to remove
the Channel Bar.

■ A dialog box may
appear, asking if you
want the Channel Bar
to appear the next time
you start your computer.

3 To display the Channel
Bar the next time you start
your computer, move the
mouse ⌖ over **Yes** and
then press the left button.

START A PROGRAM

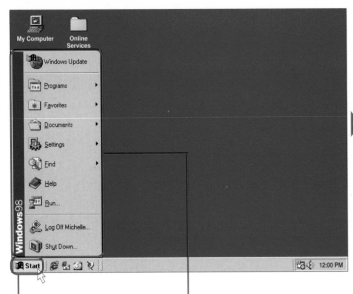

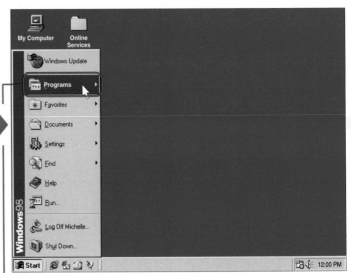

1 To display the Start menu, move the mouse ⃗ over **Start** and then press the left button.

Note: To display the Start menu using the keyboard, press and hold down the `Ctrl` *key and then press the* `Esc` *key.*

■ The Start menu appears.

2 To display the programs available on your computer, move the mouse ⃗ over **Programs**.

*Note: To select a menu item using the keyboard, press the key for the underlined letter (example: **P** for **P**rograms).*

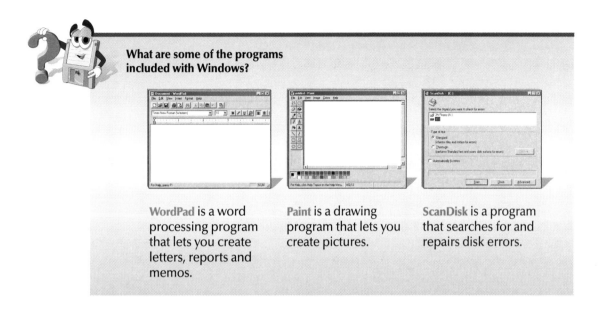

What are some of the programs included with Windows?

WordPad is a word processing program that lets you create letters, reports and memos.

Paint is a drawing program that lets you create pictures.

ScanDisk is a program that searches for and repairs disk errors.

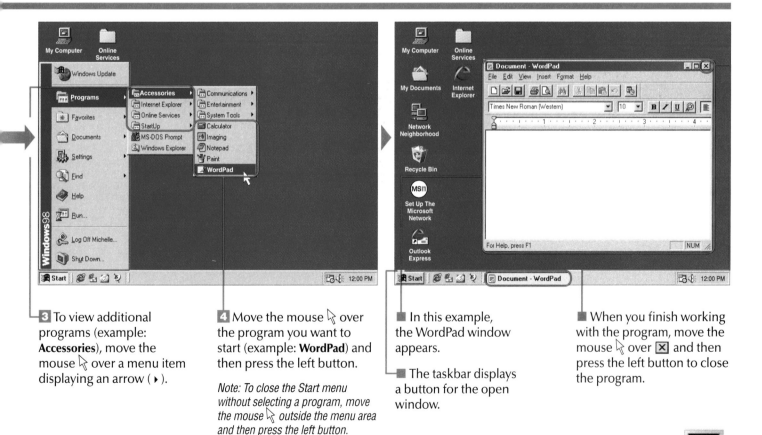

3 To view additional programs (example: **Accessories**), move the mouse ⌖ over a menu item displaying an arrow (▸).

4 Move the mouse ⌖ over the program you want to start (example: **WordPad**) and then press the left button.

Note: To close the Start menu without selecting a program, move the mouse ⌖ outside the menu area and then press the left button.

■ In this example, the WordPad window appears.

■ The taskbar displays a button for the open window.

■ When you finish working with the program, move the mouse ⌖ over ⊠ and then press the left button to close the program.

You can enlarge a window to fill your screen. This lets you view more of the window's contents.

MAXIMIZE A WINDOW

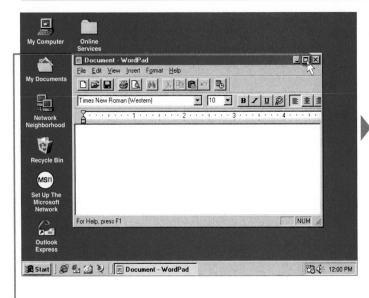

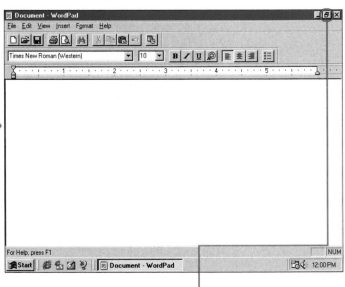

1 Move the mouse ![cursor] over ![maximize icon] in the window you want to maximize and then press the left button.

■ The window fills your screen.

■ To return the window to its previous size, move the mouse ![cursor] over ![restore icon] and then press the left button.

If you are not using a window, you can minimize the window to remove it from your screen. You can redisplay the window at any time.

MINIMIZE A WINDOW

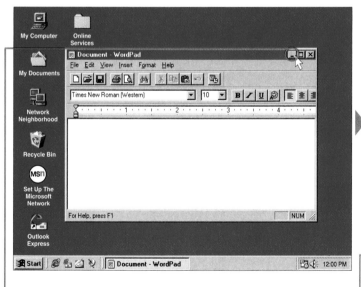

1 Move the mouse ⌇ over ▬ in the window you want to minimize and then press the left button.

■ The window reduces to a button on the taskbar.

■ To redisplay the window, move the mouse ⌇ over its button on the taskbar and then press the left button.

MOVE A WINDOW

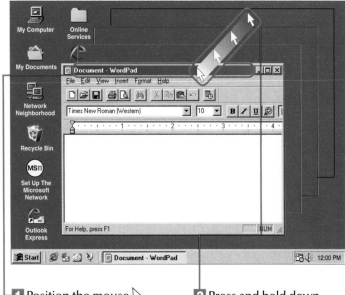

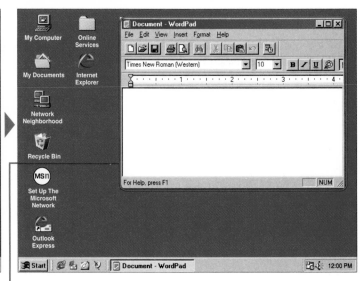

1 Position the mouse over the title bar of the window you want to move.

2 Press and hold down the left button as you drag the mouse to where you want to place the window.

■ The window moves to the new location.

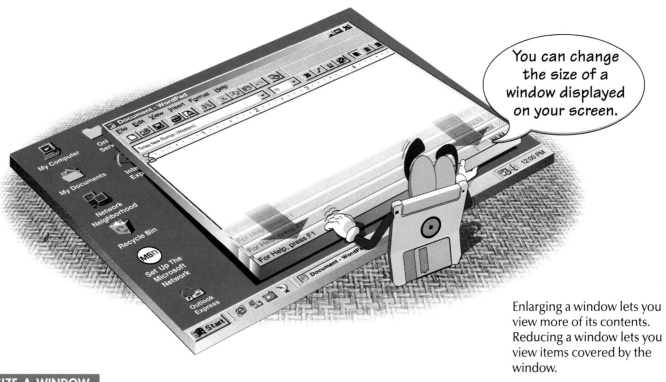

You can change the size of a window displayed on your screen.

Enlarging a window lets you view more of its contents. Reducing a window lets you view items covered by the window.

SIZE A WINDOW

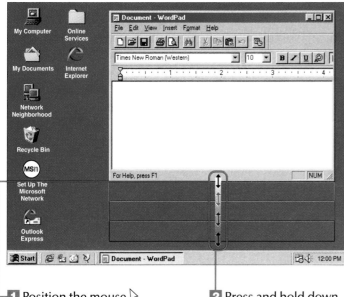

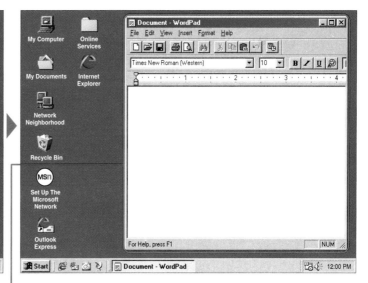

1 Position the mouse ⃗ over an edge of the window you want to size (⃗ changes to ↕, ↔ or ⬉).

2 Press and hold down the left button as you drag the mouse ↕ until the window displays the size you want.

■ The window displays the new size.

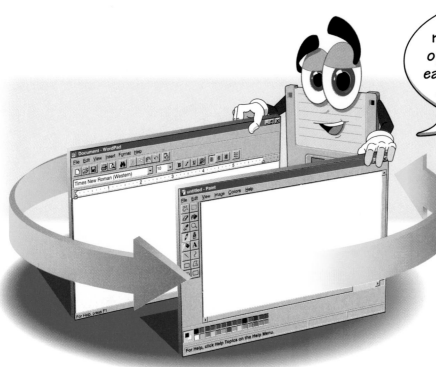

You can have more than one window open at a time. You can easily switch between all of the open windows.

Each window is like a separate piece of paper. Switching between windows is similar to placing a different piece of paper at the top of the pile.

SWITCH BETWEEN WINDOWS

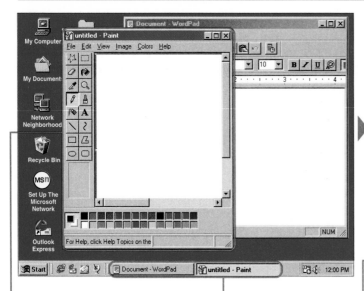

■ You can work in only one window at a time. The active window appears in front of all other windows and displays a blue title bar.

■ The taskbar displays a button for each open window.

1 To display the window you want to work with in front of all other windows, move the mouse ⬚ over its button on the taskbar and then press the left button.

■ The window appears in front of all other windows. You can now clearly view the contents of the window.

When you finish working with a window, you can close the window to remove it from your screen.

CLOSE A WINDOW

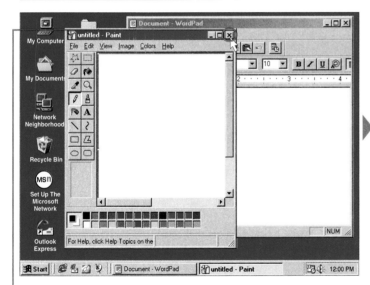

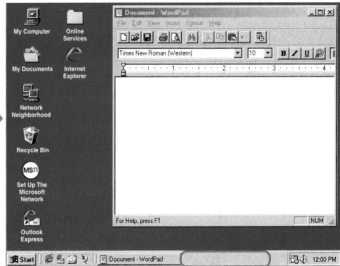

1 Move the mouse ⬚ over ⊠ in the window you want to close and then press the left button.

■ The window disappears from your screen.

■ The button for the window disappears from the taskbar.

If you have several windows open, some of them may be hidden from view. The Cascade feature lets you display your open windows one on top of the other.

CASCADE WINDOWS

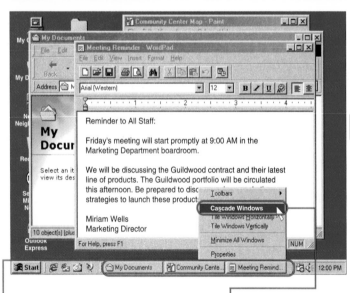

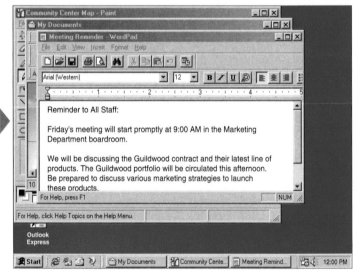

1 Move the mouse ⩗ over a blank area on the taskbar and then press the **right** button. A menu appears.

2 Move the mouse ⩗ over **Cascade Windows** and then press the left button.

■ The windows neatly overlap each other.

You can use the Tile feature to view the contents of all your open windows at once.

TILE WINDOWS

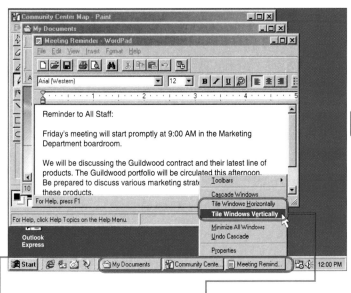

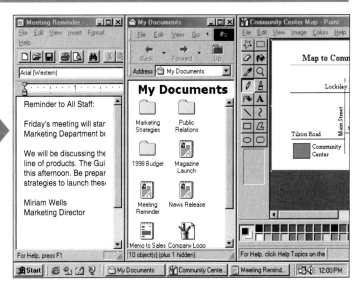

1 Move the mouse ☟ over a blank area on the taskbar and then press the **right** button. A menu appears.

2 Move the mouse ☟ over the Tile option you want to use and then press the left button.

■ You can now view the contents of all your open windows.

You can instantly minimize all your open windows to remove them from your screen. This allows you to clearly view the desktop.

SHOW THE DESKTOP

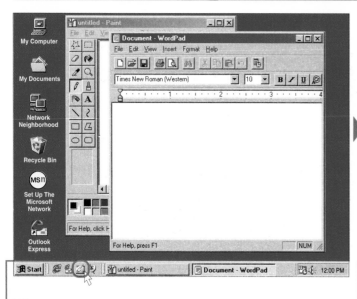

1 To minimize all the open windows on your screen, move the mouse ⟲ over 📄 and then press the left button.

■ Each window minimizes to a button on the taskbar. You can now clearly view the desktop.

■ To redisplay a window, move the mouse ⟲ over its button on the taskbar and then press the left button.

When you finish using your computer, shut down Windows before turning off the computer.

It's now safe to turn off your computer.

■ Do not turn off your computer until this message appears on your screen.

SHUT DOWN WINDOWS

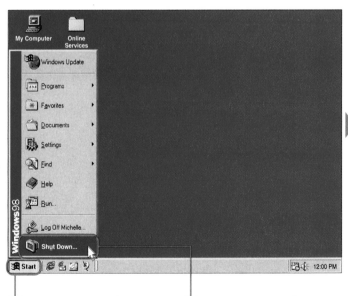

1 Move the mouse ⯑ over **Start** and then press the left button.

2 Move the mouse ⯑ over **Shut Down** and then press the left button.

■ The Shut Down Windows dialog box appears.

3 Move the mouse ⯑ over **Shut down** and then press the left button (○ changes to ⊙).

4 To shut down your computer, move the mouse ⯑ over **OK** and then press the left button.

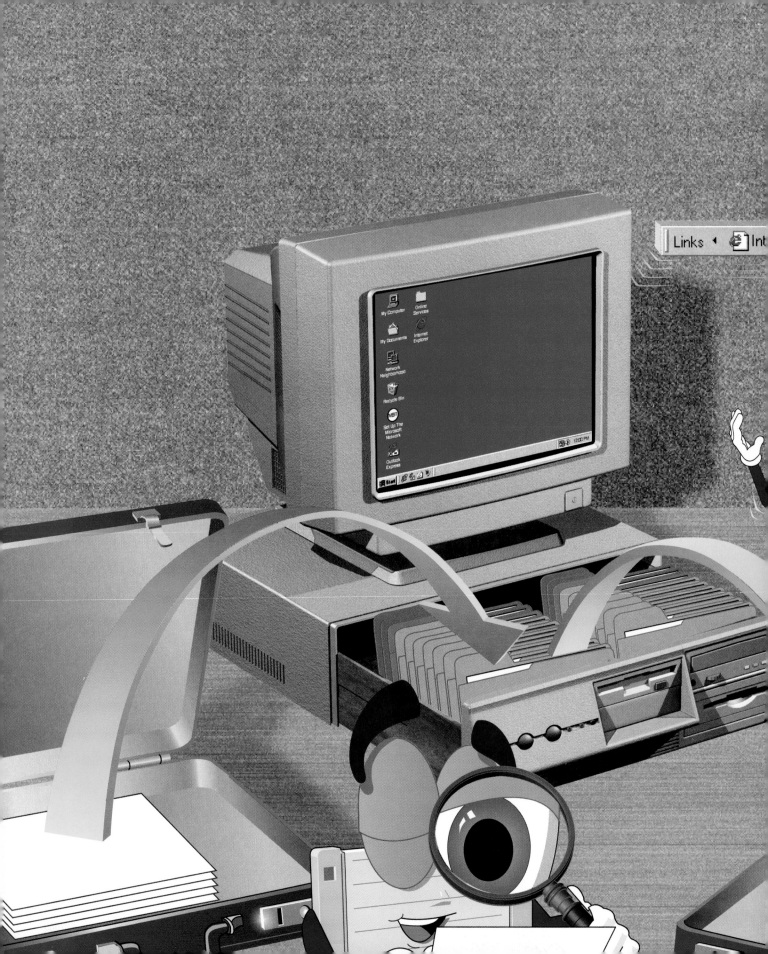

CHAPTER 2

WORK WITH FILES

Are you wondering how to work with the files stored on your computer? In this chapter you will learn how to display hidden files, transfer files between computers and more.

You can easily view the folders and files stored on your computer.

Like a filing cabinet, your computer uses folders to organize information.

VIEW CONTENTS OF YOUR COMPUTER

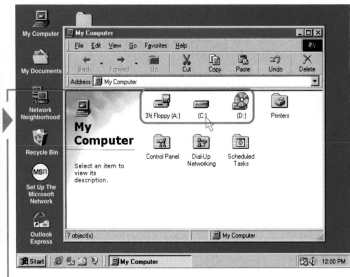

1 To view the contents of your computer, move the mouse ⬚ over **My Computer** and then quickly press the left button twice.

■ The My Computer window appears.

■ A button appears on the taskbar for the open window.

■ These items represent the drives on your computer.

2 To display the contents of a drive, move the mouse ⬚ over the drive and then quickly press the left button twice.

Note: If you want to view the contents of a floppy or CD-ROM drive, make sure you insert a floppy disk or CD-ROM disc before performing step 2.

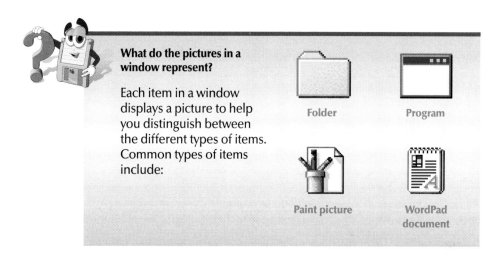

What do the pictures in a window represent?

Each item in a window displays a picture to help you distinguish between the different types of items. Common types of items include:

Folder

Program

Paint picture

WordPad document

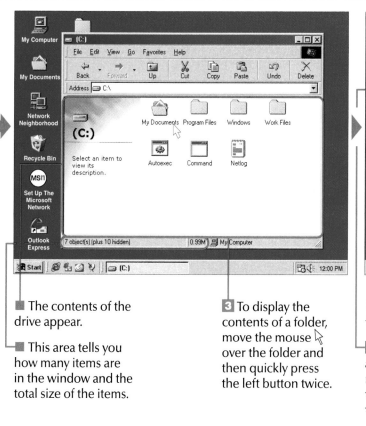

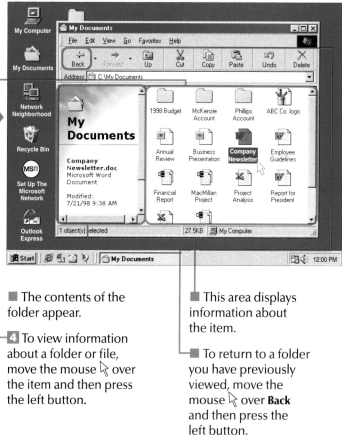

■ The contents of the drive appear.

■ This area tells you how many items are in the window and the total size of the items.

3 To display the contents of a folder, move the mouse over the folder and then quickly press the left button twice.

■ The contents of the folder appear.

4 To view information about a folder or file, move the mouse over the item and then press the left button.

■ This area displays information about the item.

■ To return to a folder you have previously viewed, move the mouse over **Back** and then press the left button.

Windows offers several toolbars that you can display or hide at any time. Toolbars allow you to quickly access commonly used commands and features.

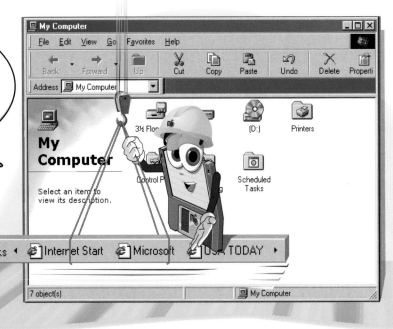

DISPLAY OR HIDE A TOOLBAR

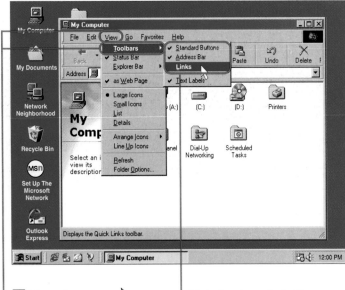

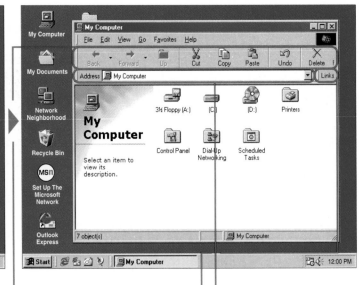

1 Move the mouse ⟍ over **View** and then press the left button.

2 Move the mouse ⟍ over **Toolbars**.

■ A check mark (✔) appears beside the name of each toolbar that is currently displayed.

3 Move the mouse ⟍ over the toolbar you want to display or hide and then press the left button.

■ The Standard Buttons toolbar displays buttons for commonly used menu commands.

■ The Address Bar toolbar displays the location of the open folder and allows you to quickly open another drive or folder.

■ The Links toolbar provides a quick way to access useful Web pages.

If a program suddenly stops working, you can close the program without shutting down Windows.

CLOSE A MISBEHAVING PROGRAM

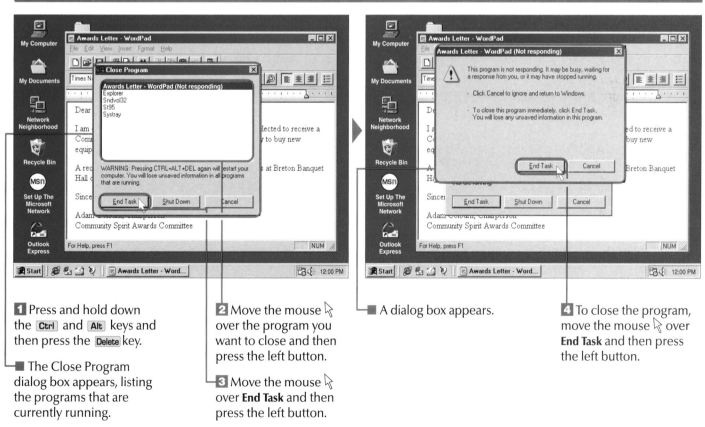

1 Press and hold down the **Ctrl** and **Alt** keys and then press the **Delete** key.

◼ The Close Program dialog box appears, listing the programs that are currently running.

2 Move the mouse ⬉ over the program you want to close and then press the left button.

3 Move the mouse ⬉ over **End Task** and then press the left button.

◼ A dialog box appears.

4 To close the program, move the mouse ⬉ over **End Task** and then press the left button.

You can instantly create, name and store a new file in the appropriate location without starting any programs.

You can focus on the organization of your files rather than the programs you need to accomplish your tasks.

CREATE A NEW FILE

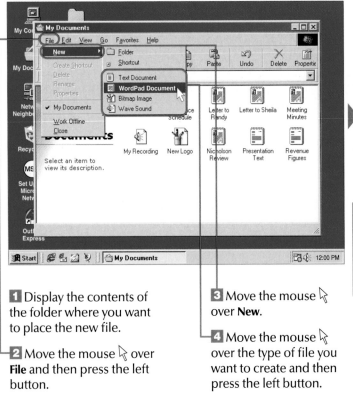

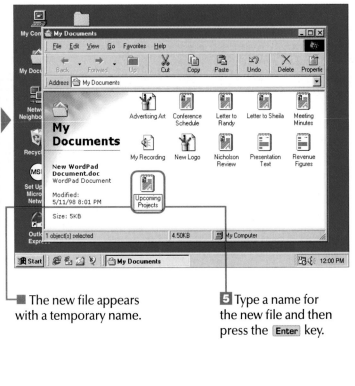

1 Display the contents of the folder where you want to place the new file.

2 Move the mouse ⇖ over **File** and then press the left button.

3 Move the mouse ⇖ over **New**.

4 Move the mouse ⇖ over the type of file you want to create and then press the left button.

■ The new file appears with a temporary name.

5 Type a name for the new file and then press the Enter key.

Can I later rename a file I created?

You can give a file a new name to better describe the contents of the file. To rename a file, move the mouse ↳ over the file and then press the left button. Press the `F2` key, type a new name for the file and then press the `Enter` key.

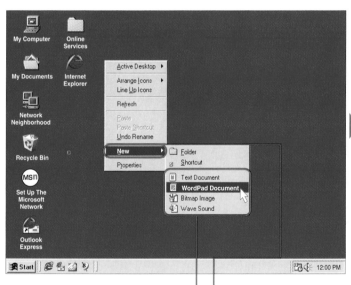

You can create a new file on your desktop.

1 Move the mouse ↳ over a blank area on your desktop and then press the **right** button. A menu appears.

2 Move the mouse ↳ over **New**.

3 Move the mouse ↳ over the type of file you want to create and then press the left button.

■ The new file appears.

4 Type a name for the new file and then press the `Enter` key.

You can review the properties of a file to learn more about the file.

DISPLAY FILE PROPERTIES

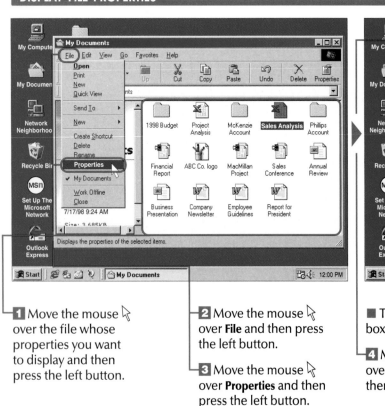

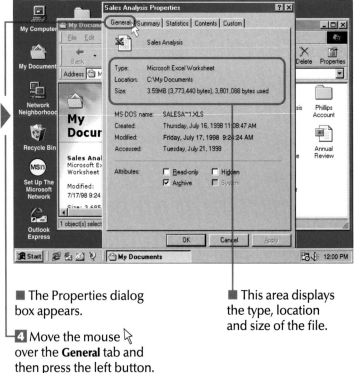

1 Move the mouse over the file whose properties you want to display and then press the left button.

2 Move the mouse over **File** and then press the left button.

3 Move the mouse over **Properties** and then press the left button.

■ The Properties dialog box appears.

4 Move the mouse over the **General** tab and then press the left button.

■ This area displays the type, location and size of the file.

How can I determine the location of a file on my computer?

The Properties dialog box shows the location, or path, of a file. A path is a list of folders you must travel through to find a file on your computer. A path starts with a drive letter and is followed by folder names. Each folder name is separated by a backslash (\).

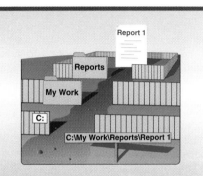

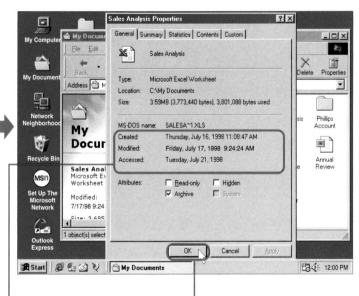

■ This area displays when you created, last changed and last opened the file.

5 When you finish reviewing the information, move the mouse ⬧ over **OK** and then press the left button to close the dialog box.

You can display the properties of a file located on your desktop.

1 Move the mouse ⬧ over the file whose properties you want to display and then press the **right** button. A menu appears.

2 Move the mouse ⬧ over **Properties** and then press the left button.

You can have Windows display or hide hidden and system files.

Hidden and system files are files that Windows and your programs need to function.

SHOW HIDDEN FILES

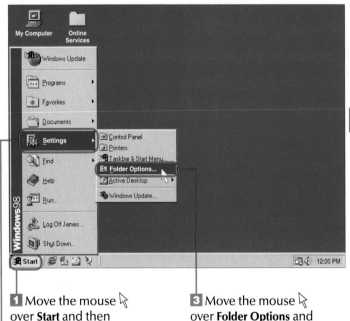

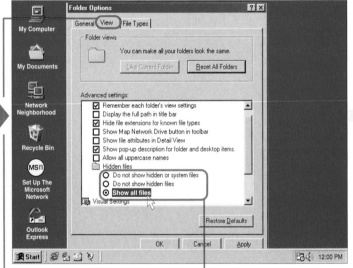

1 Move the mouse over **Start** and then press the left button.

2 Move the mouse over **Settings**.

3 Move the mouse over **Folder Options** and then press the left button.

■ The Folder Options dialog box appears.

4 Move the mouse over the **View** tab and then press the left button.

5 Move the mouse over an option to hide hidden and system files, hide only hidden files or show all files and then press the left button (○ changes to ⊙).

Should I choose to show hidden and system files?

If you choose to show hidden and system files, you may accidentally change or delete the files. This may cause your computer to no longer operate properly. To avoid problems, you should show hidden and system files only when necessary.

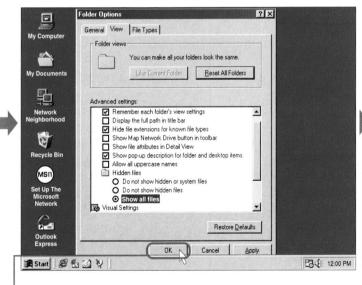

6 To confirm your change, move the mouse ▷ over **OK** and then press the left button.

■ When you view the contents of folders, the files you chose to display now appear.

■ Hidden files and folders appear dimmed.

You can play videos on your computer.

PLAY VIDEOS

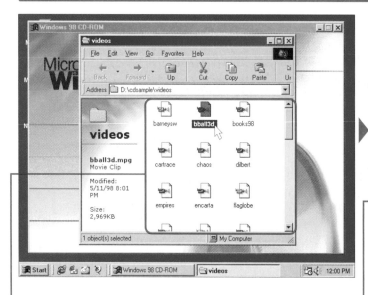

1 Move the mouse ⌖ over the video you want to play and then quickly press the left button twice.

■ A window appears and the video starts to play.

■ This area displays the total length of the video and the current position in the video.

2 Move the mouse ⌖ over one of these options to pause (▐▐) or stop (■) the play of the video and then press the left button.

Where can I get videos?

The Windows 98 CD-ROM disc includes several videos you can play. You can also get videos on the Internet or purchase videos at computer stores. Windows can play different types of videos, including videos with the .avi and .mpg extensions (example: film.mpg).

3 To once again play the video, move the mouse over ▶ and then press the left button.

4 To move through the video, position the mouse over the slider (▯). Then press and hold down the left button as you drag the slider to a new location.

5 When you finish playing the video, move the mouse over ☒ and then press the left button to close the window.

USING BRIEFCASE

Briefcase lets you work with files while you are away from the office. When you return, Briefcase will update all the files you have changed.

TRANSFER FILES TO BRIEFCASE

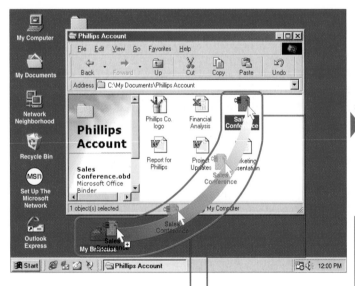

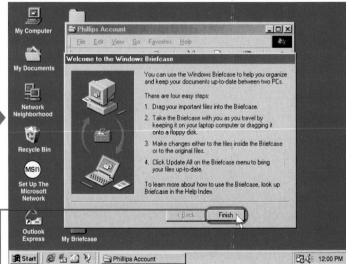

Perform the following steps on your office computer.

1 Locate a file you want to work with while away from the office.

2 Position the mouse over the file you want to transfer.

3 Press and hold down the left button as you drag the file to the Briefcase.

■ The first time you copy a file to a Briefcase, Windows displays a welcome message.

4 To close the message, move the mouse over **Finish** and then press the left button.

5 Repeat steps 1 to 3 for each file you want to work with while away from the office.

Why doesn't a Briefcase icon appear on my desktop?

If a Briefcase icon does not appear on your desktop, you may need to add the Briefcase component from the Accessories category. To add Windows components, see page 94. If Briefcase is not available in the Windows components list, Briefcase is already installed on your computer and you must create a new Briefcase icon on your desktop. See page 41 for more information.

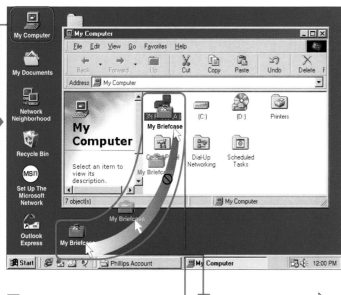

6 Insert a floppy disk into a floppy drive.

7 Move the mouse over **My Computer** and then quickly press the left button twice.

■ The My Computer window appears.

8 Position the mouse over the Briefcase.

9 Press and hold down the left button as you drag the Briefcase to the drive that contains the floppy disk.

■ Windows moves the Briefcase to the floppy disk. The Briefcase disappears from your screen.

■ You can now remove the floppy disk from the drive so you can transfer the Briefcase to your home or portable computer.

When traveling or at home, you can work with Briefcase files as you would work with any files on your computer.

WORK WITH BRIEFCASE FILES

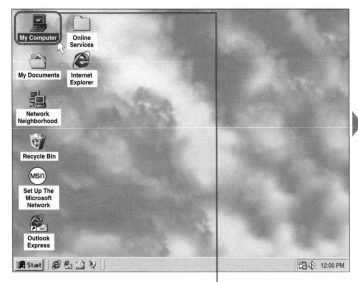

Perform the following steps on your home or portable computer.

1 Insert the floppy disk containing the Briefcase into a floppy drive.

2 Move the mouse over **My Computer** and then quickly press the left button twice.

■ The My Computer window appears.

3 Move the mouse over the drive containing the floppy disk and then quickly press the left button twice.

Can I rename the files in a Briefcase?

Do not rename the files in a Briefcase or the original files on your office computer. If you rename the files, Briefcase will not be able to update the files.

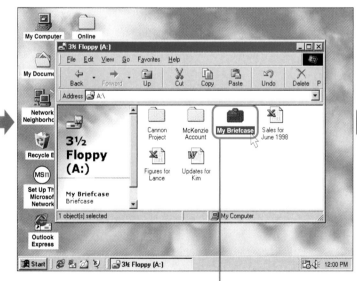

■ The contents of the floppy disk appear.

4 Move the mouse over the Briefcase and then quickly press the left button twice.

■ The contents of the Briefcase appear. You can open and edit the files in the Briefcase as you would open and edit any files.

5 When you finish working with the files, save and close the files.

6 Remove the floppy disk from the drive and return the disk to your office computer.

When you return to your office computer, you can update the files you have changed.

UPDATE BRIEFCASE FILES

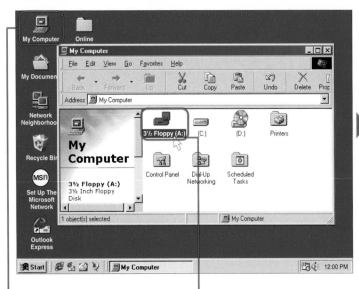

Perform the following steps on your office computer.

1 Insert the floppy disk containing the Briefcase into a floppy drive.

2 Move the mouse ⌖ over **My Computer** and then quickly press the left button twice.

■ The My Computer window appears.

3 Move the mouse ⌖ over the drive containing the floppy disk and then quickly press the left button twice.

■ The contents of the floppy disk appear.

4 Move the mouse ⌖ over the Briefcase and then quickly press the left button twice.

How does Windows know which files need to be updated?

Windows compares the files in the Briefcase to the files on your office computer to decide which files need to be updated.

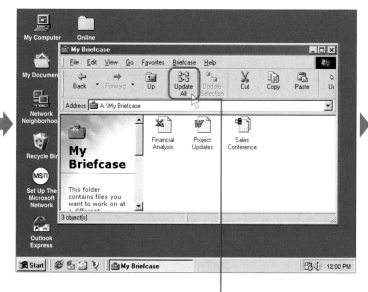

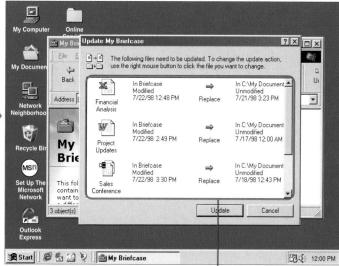

■ The contents of the Briefcase appear.

5 To update the files on your office computer, move the mouse ⬚ over **Update All** and then press the left button.

■ The Update dialog box appears.

■ This area displays the name of each file that needs to be updated and the way Windows will update each file.

CONTINUED➡

When using Briefcase, you can change the way Windows updates a file.

Replace office file with Briefcase file (➡).

Do not update file (↘).

Replace Briefcase file with office file (⬅).

UPDATE BRIEFCASE FILES (CONTINUED)

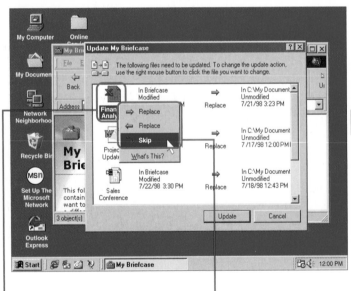

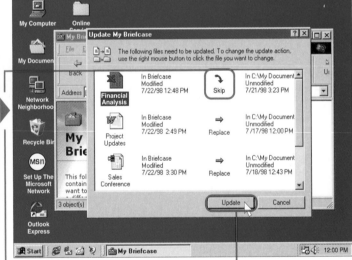

6 To change the way Windows updates a file, move the mouse ⟨ over the file and then press the **right** button. A menu appears.

7 Move the mouse ⟨ over the way you want to update the file and then press the left button.

■ Windows changes the way it will update the file.

8 Move the mouse ⟨ over **Update** and then press the left button.

■ Windows updates the files.

Can I delete a Briefcase I no longer need?

You can delete a Briefcase you no longer need. Deleting a Briefcase does not remove the original files from your computer.

Move the mouse ⌐ over the Briefcase you want to delete and then press the left button. Then press the Delete key.

CREATE A NEW BRIEFCASE

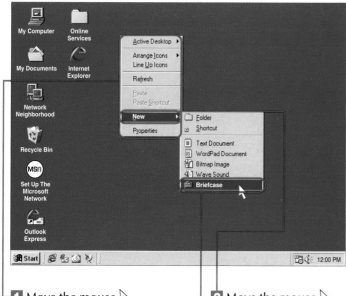

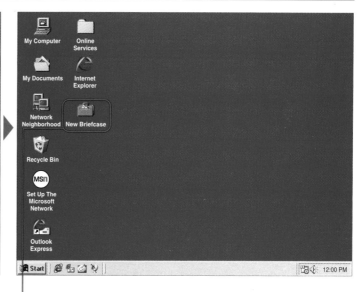

1 Move the mouse ⌐ over a blank area on your desktop and then press the **right** button. A menu appears.

2 Move the mouse ⌐ over **New**.

3 Move the mouse ⌐ over **Briefcase** and then press the left button.

■ A new Briefcase appears.

CHAPTER 3

USING WINDOWS ACCESSORIES

Would you like to create text documents, record sounds and make telephone calls with Windows 98? This chapter will show you how.

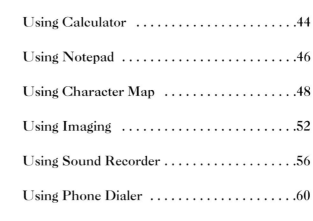

Windows provides a calculator you can use to perform calculations.

USING CALCULATOR

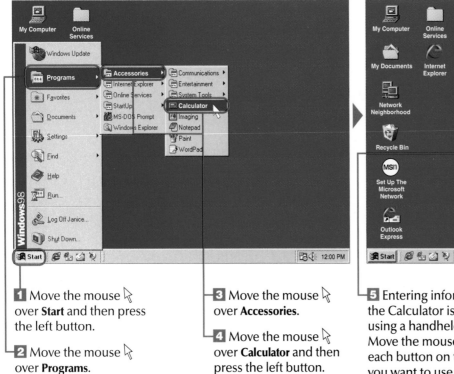

1 Move the mouse over **Start** and then press the left button.

2 Move the mouse over **Programs**.

3 Move the mouse over **Accessories**.

4 Move the mouse over **Calculator** and then press the left button.

■ The Calculator window appears.

5 Entering information into the Calculator is similar to using a handheld calculator. Move the mouse over each button on the screen you want to use and then press the left button.

■ This area displays the numbers you enter and the result of each calculation.

6 To start a new calculation, move the mouse over ☐ and then press the left button.

Can I enter information into the Calculator using the keys on the right side of my keyboard?

To enter information using the number keys on the right side of your keyboard, the Num Lock light must be on. To turn the light on, press the `Num Lock` key.

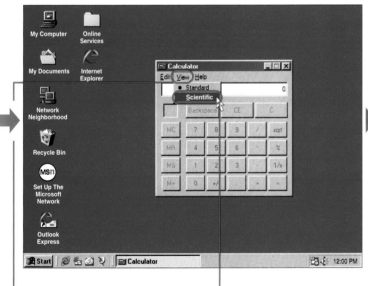

7 To change to the Scientific view of the Calculator, move the mouse over **View** and then press the left button.

8 Move the mouse over **Scientific** and then press the left button.

■ The Scientific view of the Calculator appears. You can use this view to perform more complex calculations, such as averages and exponents.

*Note: To return to the Standard view, perform steps 7 and 8, selecting **Standard** in step 8.*

9 When you finish using the Calculator, move the mouse over **X** and then press the left button to close the window.

Memo:

There will be an important [staff meeting] on Monday, October 5. Questions regarding the upcoming Halloween party will be addressed. There will be coffee and donuts so don't be late.

party hats and

staff meeting

best costume a

Notepad is a program that lets you create simple text documents.

USING NOTEPAD

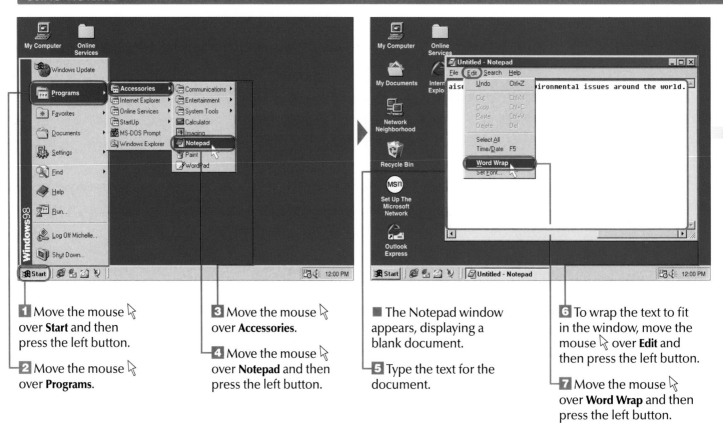

1 Move the mouse over **Start** and then press the left button.

2 Move the mouse over **Programs**.

3 Move the mouse over **Accessories**.

4 Move the mouse over **Notepad** and then press the left button.

■ The Notepad window appears, displaying a blank document.

5 Type the text for the document.

6 To wrap the text to fit in the window, move the mouse over **Edit** and then press the left button.

7 Move the mouse over **Word Wrap** and then press the left button.

Can I use Notepad to enter the current time and date into a document?

To enter the current time and date into your document, press the **F5** key. Notepad will automatically insert the time and date where the insertion point flashes on your screen.

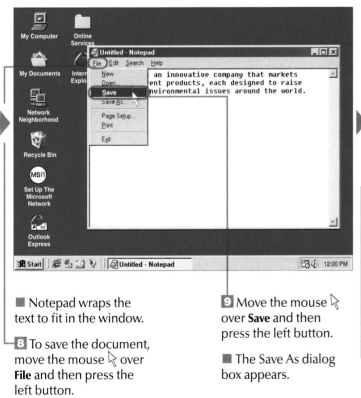

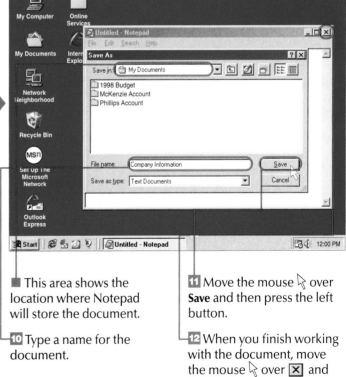

■ Notepad wraps the text to fit in the window.

8 To save the document, move the mouse ⇧ over **File** and then press the left button.

9 Move the mouse ⇧ over **Save** and then press the left button.

■ The Save As dialog box appears.

■ This area shows the location where Notepad will store the document.

10 Type a name for the document.

11 Move the mouse ⇧ over **Save** and then press the left button.

12 When you finish working with the document, move the mouse ⇧ over ☒ and then press the left button to close the document.

When creating documents, you can use Character Map to include special characters that are not available on your keyboard.

If the Character Map feature is not available, you need to add the Character Map component from the System Tools category. To add Windows components, see page 94.

USING CHARACTER MAP

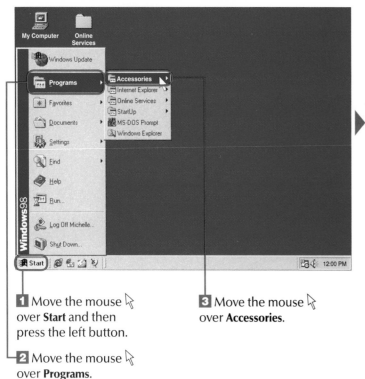

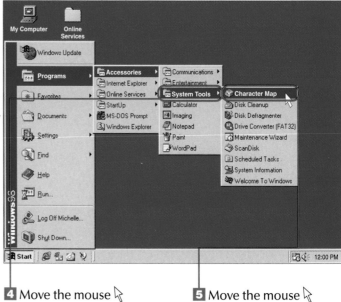

1 Move the mouse over **Start** and then press the left button.

2 Move the mouse over **Programs**.

3 Move the mouse over **Accessories**.

4 Move the mouse over **System Tools**.

5 Move the mouse over **Character Map** and then press the left button.

■ The Character Map window appears.

What special characters are available in Character Map?

Character Map offers many special characters that you can choose from, such as ©, é, ½ and ™. Each font available in Character Map provides a different collection of special characters.

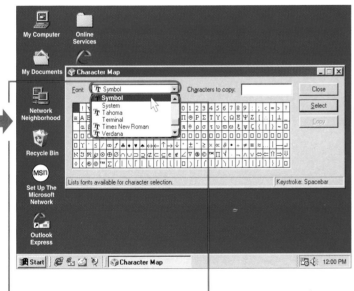

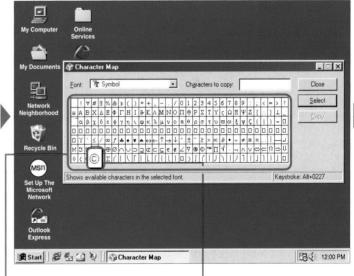

6 To list the available fonts, move the mouse over this area and then press the left button.

7 Move the mouse over the font that contains the character(s) you want to display and then press the left button.

■ This area displays the characters for the font you selected.

8 To display an enlarged version of a character, position the mouse over the character and then press and hold down the left button.

CONTINUED

> You can copy the special characters from Character Map and place them in your documents.

USING CHARACTER MAP (CONTINUED)

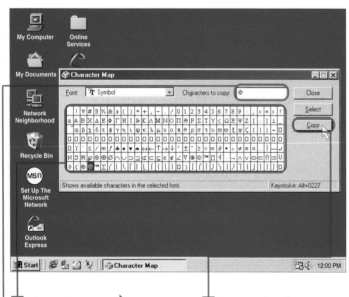

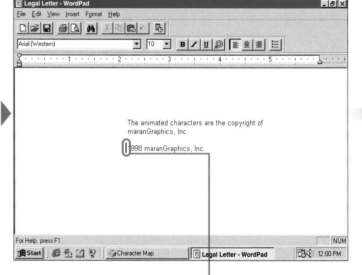

9 Move the mouse over each character you want to use in a document and then quickly press the left button twice.

■ This area displays each character you select.

10 To copy the character(s) you selected, move the mouse over **Copy** and then press the left button.

11 Open the document you want to display the character(s).

12 Position the insertion point where you want the character(s) to appear.

How can I quickly enter special characters into my documents?

Each special character has a keystroke combination that allows you to quickly enter the character into a document. The keystroke combination for the selected character appears at the bottom right corner of the Character Map window.

Keystroke: Alt+0227

If the keystroke combination includes numbers, you must enter the numbers using the numeric keypad on your keyboard.

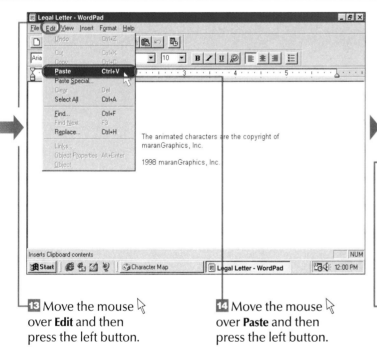

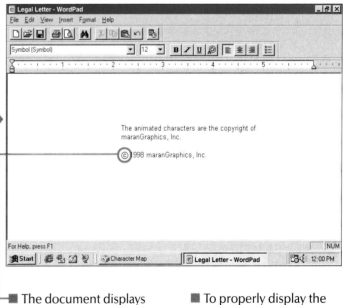

13 Move the mouse over **Edit** and then press the left button.

14 Move the mouse over **Paste** and then press the left button.

■ The document displays the character(s).

■ To properly display the character(s), make sure the font in the document matches the font you selected in Character Map in step 7.

You can use Imaging to work with scanned documents.

You need a scanner to transfer paper documents to your computer.

USING IMAGING

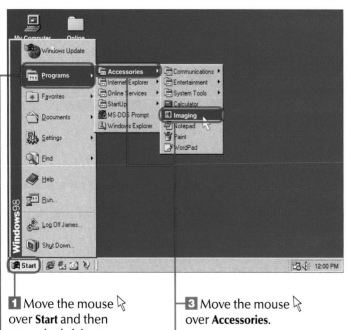

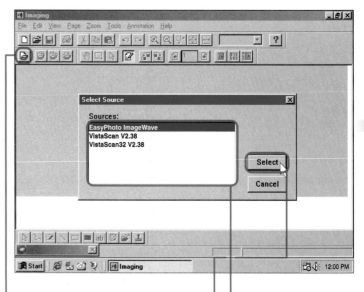

1 Move the mouse over **Start** and then press the left button.

2 Move the mouse over **Programs**.

3 Move the mouse over **Accessories**.

4 Move the mouse over **Imaging** and then press the left button.

■ The Imaging window appears.

SCAN A NEW DOCUMENT

1 To scan a new document, move the mouse over 🖹 and then press the left button.

■ The Select Source dialog box may appear the first time you scan a document.

2 Move the mouse over the scanner you want to use and then press the left button.

3 Move the mouse over **Select** and then press the left button.

52

Why would I want to scan a document?

You may want to scan documents such as forms, receipts, pictures or newspaper clippings. You will be able to access the scanned documents on your computer much faster than paper documents on your desk or in your filing cabinet. You can also send scanned documents to friends and colleagues in e-mail messages.

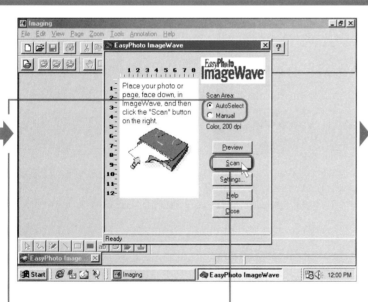

■ The program you use to scan your documents opens.

4 Set the appropriate options for your scan. You may need to refer to the documentation that came with your scanner.

5 Move the mouse over the button that allows you to scan the document and then press the left button.

■ The scanned document appears.

6 If the document appears upside down, move the mouse over one of the following options and then press the left button.

Rotate document to the left

Rotate document to the right

You can magnify or reduce the size of a document in Imaging.

MAGNIFY OR REDUCE A DOCUMENT

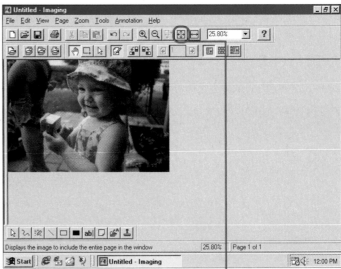

1 To magnify or reduce the size of a document, move the mouse ⍟ over one of the following options and then press the left button.

🔍 Magnify

🔍 Reduce

■ The document displays the new size.

■ To view the entire document on your screen, move the mouse ⍟ over 🖼 and then press the left button.

You can add a note to an Imaging document.

Information you add to an Imaging document is called an annotation.

ADD A NOTE

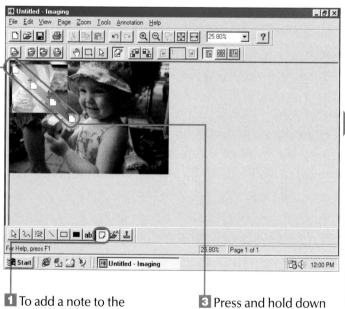

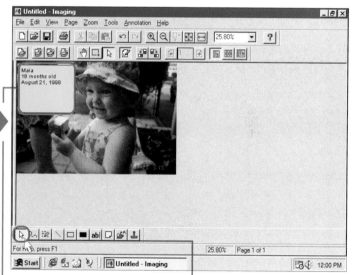

1 To add a note to the document, move the mouse ⟡ over ▯ and then press the left button.

2 Position the mouse ⟡ where you want the top left edge of the note to appear (⟡ changes to ⁺▯).

3 Press and hold down the left button as you drag the mouse ⁺▯ until the note displays the size you want.

4 Type the text for the note.

5 When you finish typing the text, move the mouse ⟡ over ▣ and then press the left button.

■ To delete the note, move the mouse ⟡ over the note and then press the left button. Then press the Delete key.

You can use Sound Recorder to record your own sounds.

You need a sound card and speakers to record and play sounds.

USING SOUND RECORDER

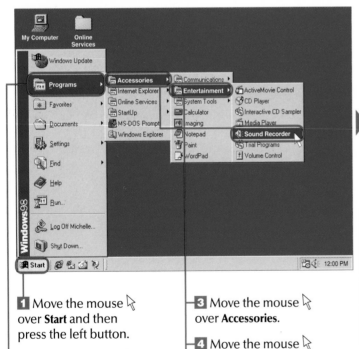

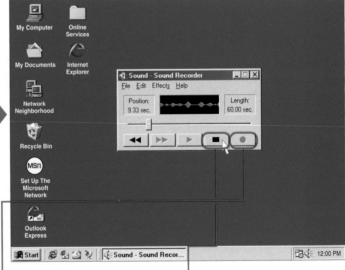

1 Move the mouse over **Start** and then press the left button.

2 Move the mouse over **Programs**.

3 Move the mouse over **Accessories**.

4 Move the mouse over **Entertainment**.

5 Move the mouse over **Sound Recorder** and then press the left button.

■ The Sound Recorder window appears.

6 To start recording, move the mouse over ● and then press the left button.

7 Use your microphone or other sound device to record sounds.

8 To stop recording, move the mouse over ■ and then press the left button.

What devices can I use to record sounds?

You can record sounds from a microphone, CD player, stereo, VCR or any other sound device connected to your computer.

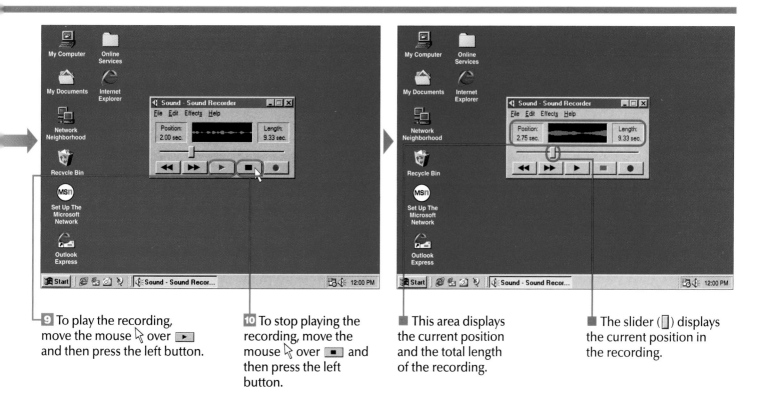

9 To play the recording, move the mouse over ▶ and then press the left button.

10 To stop playing the recording, move the mouse over ■ and then press the left button.

■ This area displays the current position and the total length of the recording.

■ The slider ( ) displays the current position in the recording.

Sound Recorder offers several sound effects you can use to change your recording.

You can adjust the volume, adjust the speed, add an echo or play a recording in reverse.

USING SOUND RECORDER (CONTINUED)

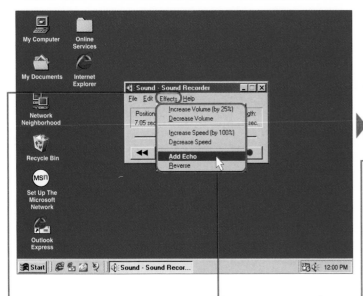

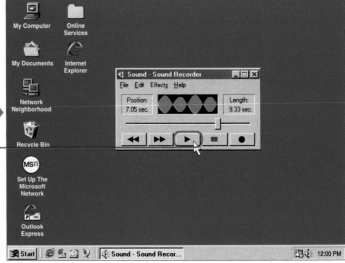

ADD A SOUND EFFECT

1 To add a special sound effect to a recording, move the mouse ⬚ over **Effects** and then press the left button.

2 Move the mouse ⬚ over the sound effect you want to use and then press the left button.

3 To play the recording and hear the sound effect, move the mouse ⬚ over ▶ and then press the left button.

■ You can repeat steps **1** and **2** for each sound effect you want to use.

How can I play a recording I saved?

Recordings you have saved display a specific icon ( ) on your computer. To play a recording, move the mouse over the icon and then quickly press the left button twice.

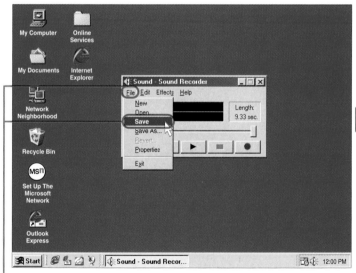

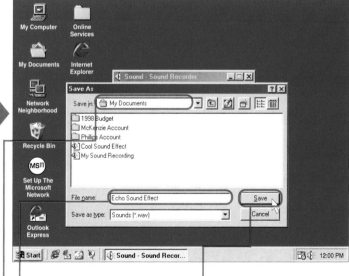

SAVE A RECORDING

1 Move the mouse over **File** and then press the left button.

2 Move the mouse over **Save** and then press the left button.

■ The Save As dialog box appears.

Note: If you previously saved the recording, the Save As dialog box will not appear since you have already named the recording.

3 Type a name for your recording.

■ This area shows where Windows will save the recording.

4 To save the recording, move the mouse over **Save** and then press the left button.

You can use Phone Dialer to make telephone calls from your computer.

Before you can use Phone Dialer, you need to connect a telephone to your modem.

USING PHONE DIALER

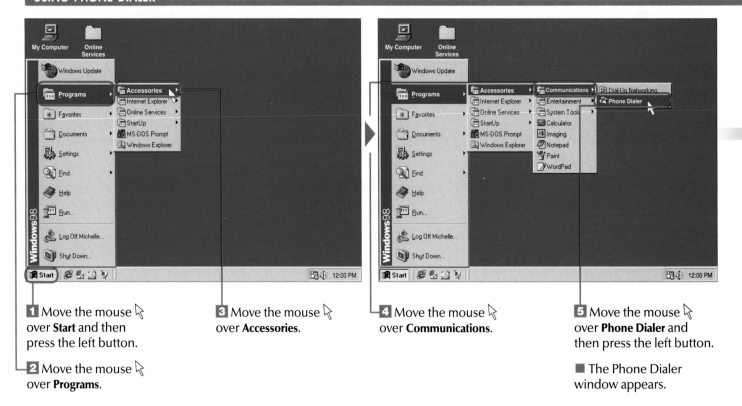

1 Move the mouse ▷ over **Start** and then press the left button.

2 Move the mouse ▷ over **Programs**.

3 Move the mouse ▷ over **Accessories**.

4 Move the mouse ▷ over **Communications**.

5 Move the mouse ▷ over **Phone Dialer** and then press the left button.

■ The Phone Dialer window appears.

How do I connect a telephone to my modem?

Plug the telephone cord into the jack labeled "Phone" on your modem. If you have an internal modem, you will be able to see the edge of the modem at the back of your computer.

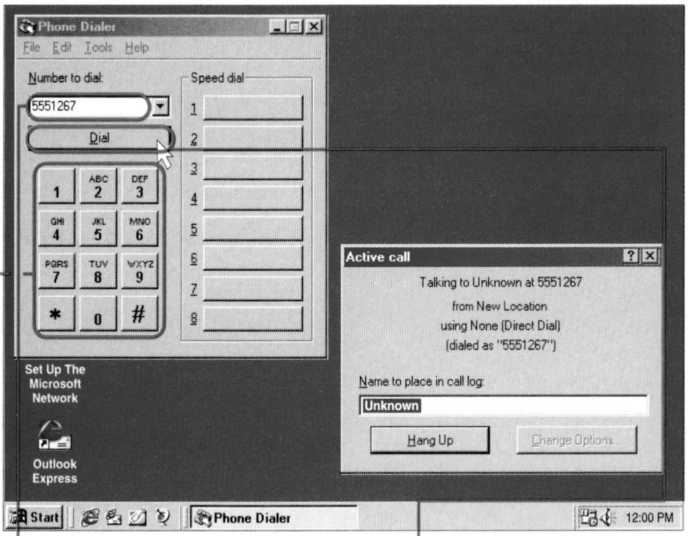

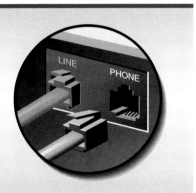

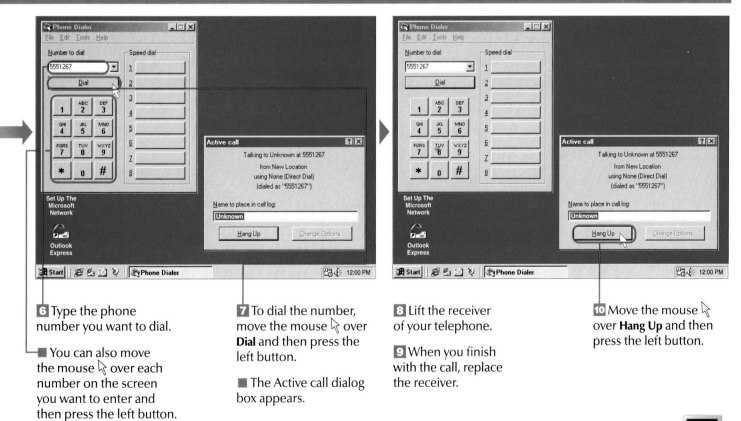

6 Type the phone number you want to dial.

■ You can also move the mouse over each number on the screen you want to enter and then press the left button.

7 To dial the number, move the mouse over **Dial** and then press the left button.

■ The Active call dialog box appears.

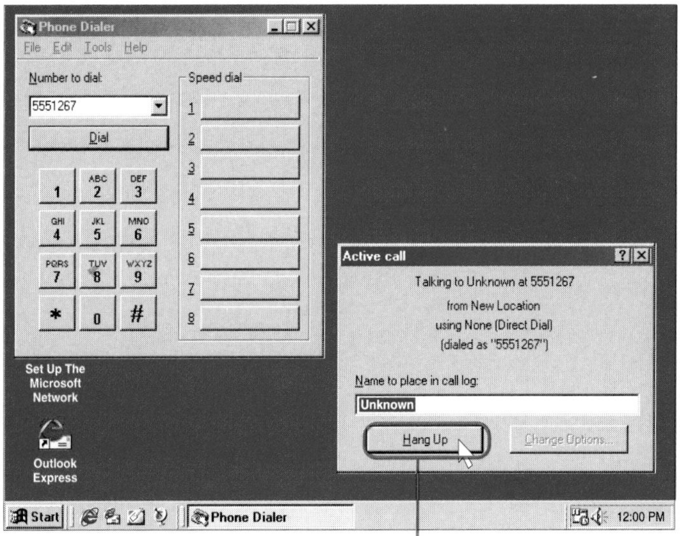

8 Lift the receiver of your telephone.

9 When you finish with the call, replace the receiver.

10 Move the mouse over **Hang Up** and then press the left button.

You can store phone numbers you frequently use on speed-dial buttons.

STORE A PHONE NUMBER

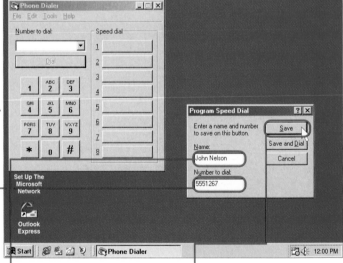

1 To store a phone number, move the mouse ⏵ over a blank speed-dial button and then press the left button.

■ The Program Speed Dial dialog box appears.

2 Type the name of the person whose phone number you want to store.

3 Move the mouse ⏵ over this area and then press the left button. Then type the person's phone number.

4 To store the information, move the mouse ⏵ over **Save** and then press the left button.

Can I use the telephone and browse the Web at the same time?

No. Although you can use the same phone line to talk on the telephone and browse the Web, you cannot perform both tasks at the same time.

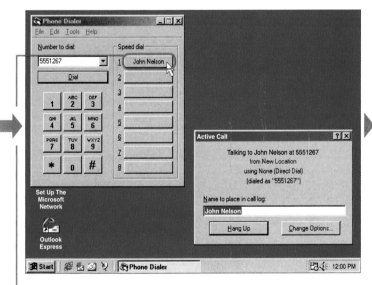

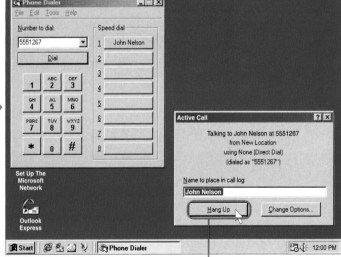

■ The name appears on the button.

5 To dial a stored phone number, move the mouse ⇩ over the speed-dial button for the number you want to dial and then press the left button.

■ The Active call dialog box appears.

6 Lift the receiver of your telephone.

7 When you finish with the call, replace the receiver.

8 Move the mouse ⇩ over **Hang Up** and then press the left button.

CHAPTER 4

CUSTOMIZE WINDOWS

Would you like to customize the way Windows 98 looks and acts? This chapter teaches you how to change the appearance of your folders, start programs automatically and add items to the Start menu.

You can hide the taskbar to give you more room on the screen to accomplish tasks.

HIDE THE TASKBAR

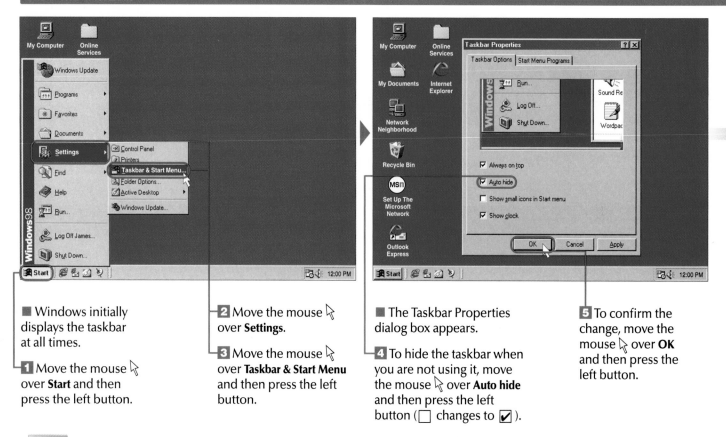

■ Windows initially displays the taskbar at all times.

1 Move the mouse over **Start** and then press the left button.

2 Move the mouse over **Settings**.

3 Move the mouse over **Taskbar & Start Menu** and then press the left button.

■ The Taskbar Properties dialog box appears.

4 To hide the taskbar when you are not using it, move the mouse over **Auto hide** and then press the left button (□ changes to ☑).

5 To confirm the change, move the mouse over **OK** and then press the left button.

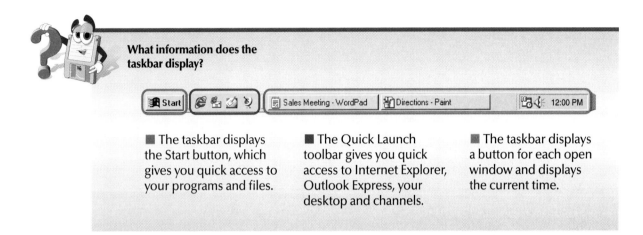

What information does the taskbar display?

■ The taskbar displays the Start button, which gives you quick access to your programs and files.

■ The Quick Launch toolbar gives you quick access to Internet Explorer, Outlook Express, your desktop and channels.

■ The taskbar displays a button for each open window and displays the current time.

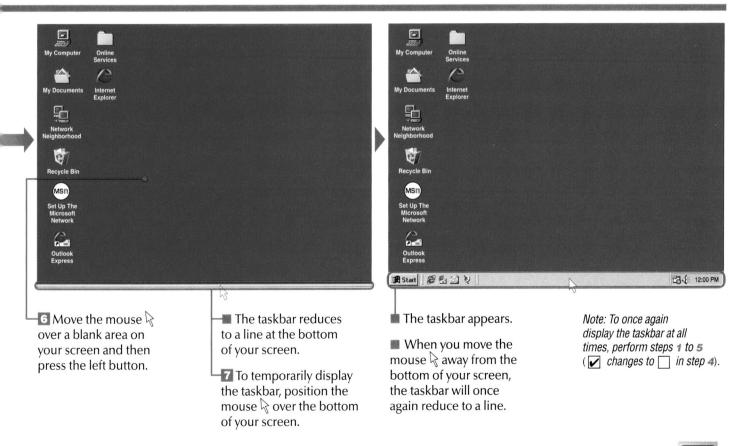

6 Move the mouse ⬚ over a blank area on your screen and then press the left button.

■ The taskbar reduces to a line at the bottom of your screen.

7 To temporarily display the taskbar, position the mouse ⬚ over the bottom of your screen.

■ The taskbar appears.

■ When you move the mouse ⬚ away from the bottom of your screen, the taskbar will once again reduce to a line.

Note: To once again display the taskbar at all times, perform steps 1 to 5 (✔ changes to ☐ in step 4).

Windows includes several ready-made toolbars that you can add to the taskbar. Toolbars provide instant access to commands and features.

ADD A TOOLBAR TO THE TASKBAR

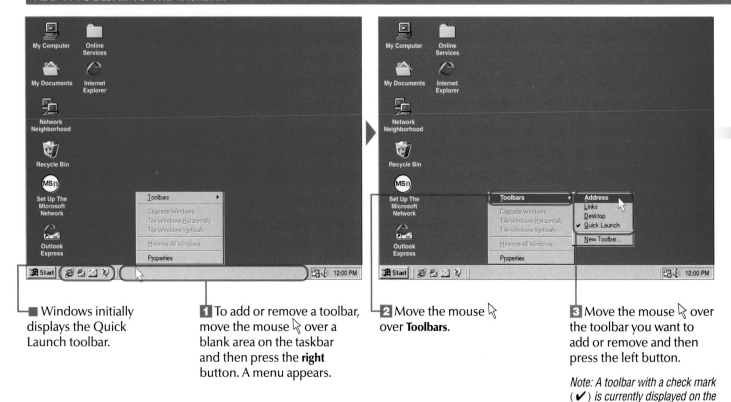

■ Windows initially displays the Quick Launch toolbar.

1 To add or remove a toolbar, move the mouse ⌖ over a blank area on the taskbar and then press the **right** button. A menu appears.

2 Move the mouse ⌖ over **Toolbars**.

3 Move the mouse ⌖ over the toolbar you want to add or remove and then press the left button.

Note: A toolbar with a check mark (✔) is currently displayed on the taskbar.

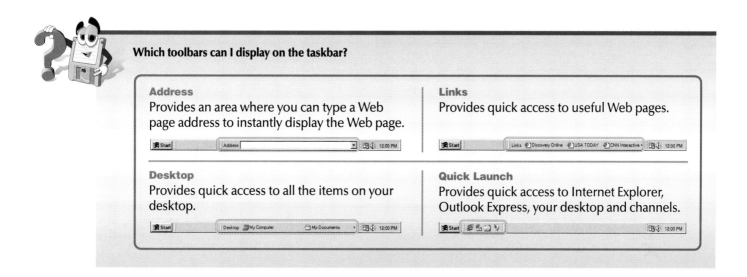

Which toolbars can I display on the taskbar?

Address
Provides an area where you can type a Web page address to instantly display the Web page.

Links
Provides quick access to useful Web pages.

Desktop
Provides quick access to all the items on your desktop.

Quick Launch
Provides quick access to Internet Explorer, Outlook Express, your desktop and channels.

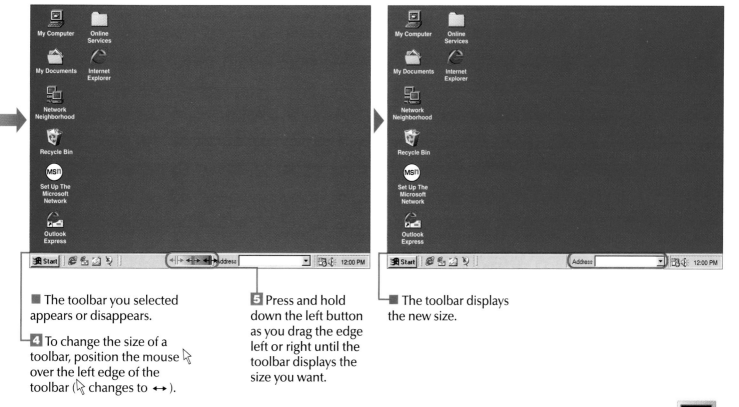

■ The toolbar you selected appears or disappears.

4 To change the size of a toolbar, position the mouse ⦰ over the left edge of the toolbar (⦰ changes to ↔).

5 Press and hold down the left button as you drag the edge left or right until the toolbar displays the size you want.

■ The toolbar displays the new size.

You can customize the appearance of a folder by adding a background picture.

Other Background Pictures Available

CHANGE FOLDER APPEARANCE

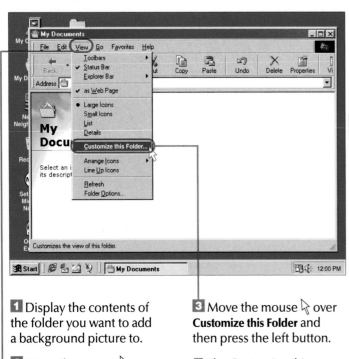

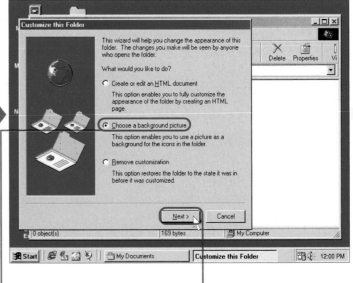

1 Display the contents of the folder you want to add a background picture to.

2 Move the mouse ⯬ over **View** and then press the left button.

3 Move the mouse ⯬ over **Customize this Folder** and then press the left button.

■ The Customize this Folder wizard appears.

4 To add a background picture to the folder, move the mouse ⯬ over this option and then press the left button (○ changes to ⊙).

5 To continue, move the mouse ⯬ over **Next** and then press the left button.

Can I add a background picture to any folder on my computer?

You cannot add a background picture to some folders on your computer. Folders you cannot add a background picture to include the My Computer folder, the Control Panel folder, the Printers folder and the Fonts folder.

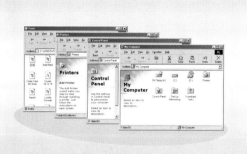

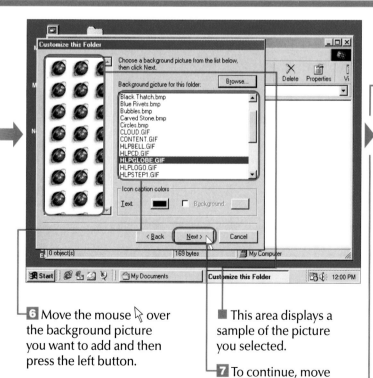

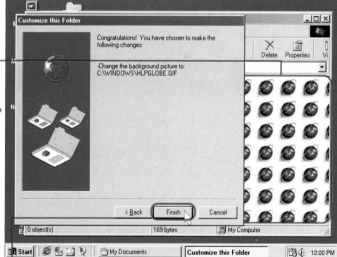

6 Move the mouse ⬚ over the background picture you want to add and then press the left button.

■ This area displays a sample of the picture you selected.

7 To continue, move the mouse ⬚ over **Next** and then press the left button.

8 To change the appearance of the folder, move the mouse ⬚ over **Finish** and then press the left button.

■ Windows adds the background picture to the folder.

■ To remove the background picture from a folder, perform steps **1** to **5**, selecting **Remove customization** in step **4**. Then perform steps **7** and **8**.

You can view the fonts available on your computer before using the fonts in your documents.

VIEW FONTS ON YOUR COMPUTER

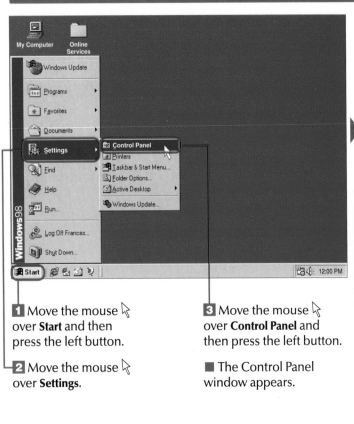

1 Move the mouse ⤴ over **Start** and then press the left button.

2 Move the mouse ⤴ over **Settings**.

3 Move the mouse ⤴ over **Control Panel** and then press the left button.

■ The Control Panel window appears.

4 Move the mouse ⤴ over **Fonts** and then quickly press the left button twice.

■ The Fonts window appears.

What types of fonts are available on my computer?

TrueType Fonts
Most of the fonts included with Windows are TrueType fonts. A TrueType font will print exactly as it appears on your screen.

System Fonts
Windows uses system fonts to display text in menus and dialog boxes.

Printer Fonts
Most printers include built-in fonts which are stored in the printer's memory. A printer font may not print as it appears on your screen. Printer fonts do not appear in the Fonts window.

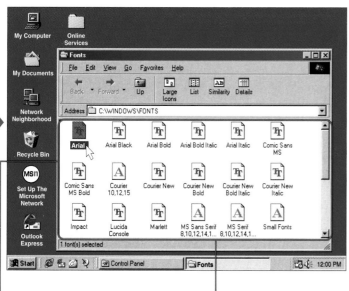

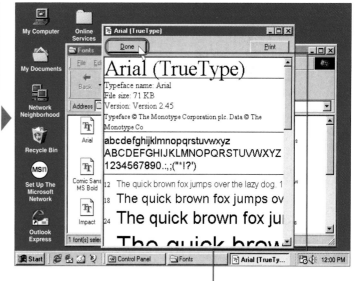

■ Each icon in the Fonts window represents a font installed on your computer.

5 Move the mouse ⏷ over a font you want to view and then quickly press the left button twice.

■ A window appears, displaying information about the font you selected and samples of the font in various sizes.

6 When you finish reviewing the information, move the mouse ⏷ over **Done** and then press the left button to close the window.

You can add fonts to your computer to give you more choices when creating documents.

ADD FONTS TO YOUR COMPUTER

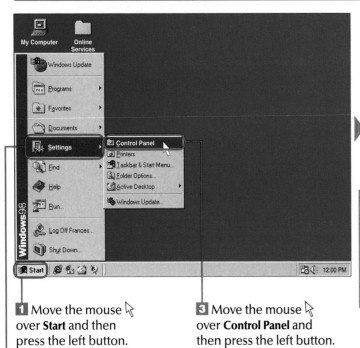

1 Move the mouse ⇗ over **Start** and then press the left button.

2 Move the mouse ⇗ over **Settings**.

3 Move the mouse ⇗ over **Control Panel** and then press the left button.

■ The Control Panel window appears.

4 Move the mouse ⇗ over **Fonts** and then quickly press the left button twice.

■ The Fonts window appears.

Where can I get fonts?

You can purchase fonts wherever computer software is sold. You can also find fonts on the Internet. Some fonts on the Internet are compressed. You can use a program, such as WinZip, to decompress the fonts so you can add them to your computer.

WinZip is available on the Web at www.winzip.com. Fonts are available at the following Web sites:

www.fontage.com

www.fontface.com

www.tyworld.com

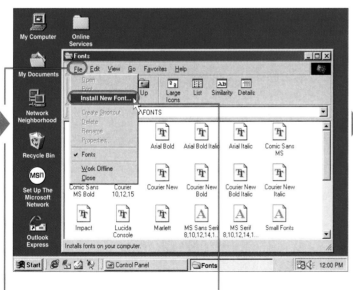

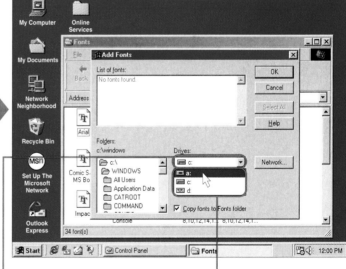

■ The Fonts window displays the fonts installed on your computer.

5 Move the mouse ⟍ over **File** and then press the left button.

6 Move the mouse ⟍ over **Install New Font** and then press the left button.

■ The Add Fonts dialog box appears.

7 To select the drive containing the fonts you want to add, move the mouse ⟍ over this area and then press the left button.

8 Move the mouse ⟍ over the drive containing the fonts and then press the left button.

CONTINUED➡

When you add fonts to your computer, you will be able to use the fonts in all of your programs.

ADD FONTS TO YOUR COMPUTER (CONTINUED)

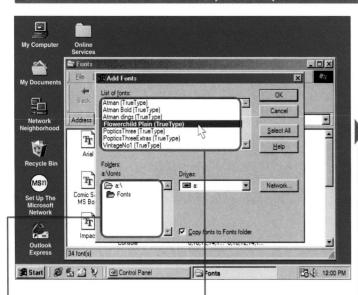

9 Move the mouse ⅄ over the folder containing the fonts and then quickly press the left button twice.

■ This area displays the fonts stored in the location you selected.

10 Move the mouse ⅄ over the font you want to add and then press the left button.

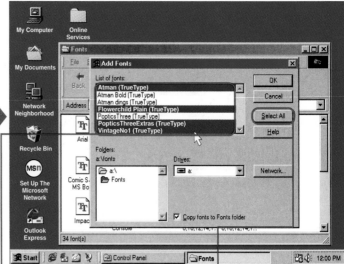

11 To select additional fonts, press and hold down the `Ctrl` key. Still holding down the `Ctrl` key, move the mouse ⅄ over each font you want to select and then press the left button.

■ To quickly select all the displayed fonts, move the mouse ⅄ over **Select All** and then press the left button.

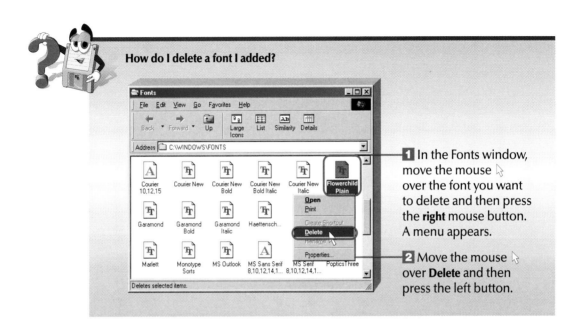

How do I delete a font I added?

1 In the Fonts window, move the mouse over the font you want to delete and then press the **right** mouse button. A menu appears.

2 Move the mouse over **Delete** and then press the left button.

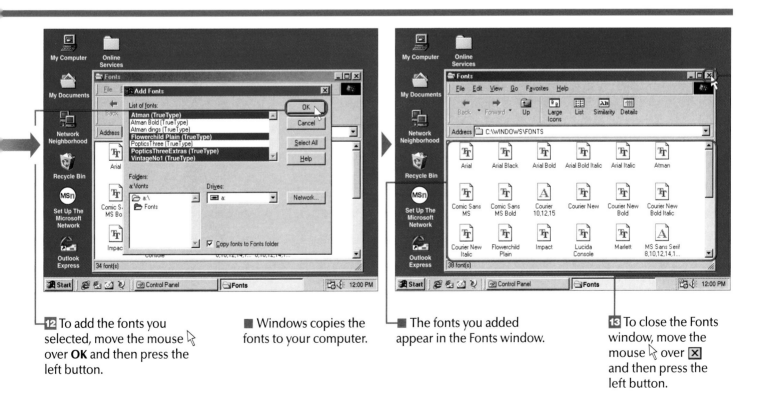

12 To add the fonts you selected, move the mouse over **OK** and then press the left button.

■ Windows copies the fonts to your computer.

■ The fonts you added appear in the Fonts window.

13 To close the Fonts window, move the mouse over ⊠ and then press the left button.

CHANGE POWER MANAGEMENT SETTINGS

Windows can reduce the power used by your computer.

Power management is useful for reducing the power used by your desktop computer or increasing the battery life of a portable computer. Some computers do not support power management features.

CHANGE POWER MANAGEMENT SETTINGS

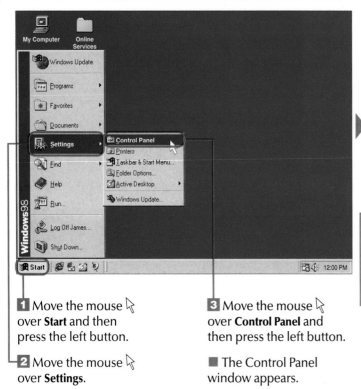

1 Move the mouse over **Start** and then press the left button.

2 Move the mouse over **Settings**.

3 Move the mouse over **Control Panel** and then press the left button.

■ The Control Panel window appears.

4 Move the mouse over **Power Management** and then quickly press the left button twice.

■ The Power Management Properties dialog box appears.

How does Windows conserve power?

Windows can conserve power by placing your computer on standby and by turning off your monitor and hard disks when you do not use the computer for a certain period of time.

You can move your mouse or press a key on your keyboard to resume working on your computer.

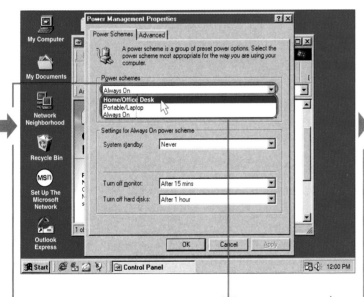

5 To list the available power schemes, move the mouse ℟ over this area and then press the left button.

6 Move the mouse ℟ over the power scheme that best describes the way you use your computer and then press the left button.

■ This area displays the amount of time your computer must be inactive before the computer goes on standby.

Note: This option may not be available.

■ This area displays the amount of time the computer must be inactive before your monitor and hard disks turn off.

7 To confirm your change, move the mouse ℟ over **OK** and then press the left button.

If you use the same program every day, you can have the program start automatically every time you turn on your computer.

Click

START A PROGRAM AUTOMATICALLY

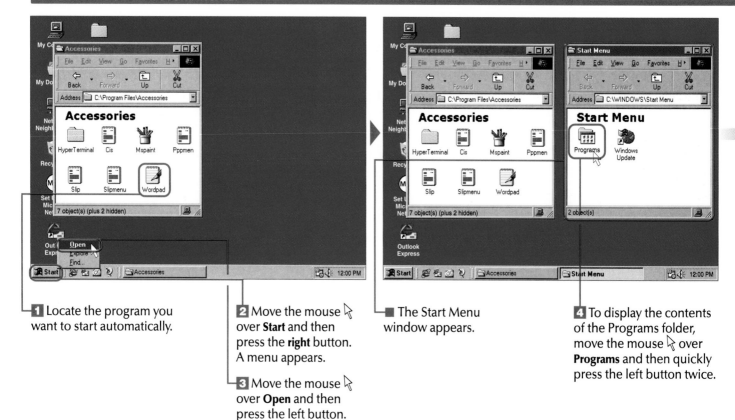

1 Locate the program you want to start automatically.

2 Move the mouse over **Start** and then press the **right** button. A menu appears.

3 Move the mouse over **Open** and then press the left button.

■ The Start Menu window appears.

4 To display the contents of the Programs folder, move the mouse over **Programs** and then quickly press the left button twice.

How do I stop a program from starting automatically?

If you no longer want a program to start automatically, delete the shortcut for the program from the StartUp folder. Deleting a shortcut from the StartUp folder will not remove the program from your computer.

Move the mouse ⍦ over the shortcut to the program you no longer want to start automatically and then press the left button. Then press the Delete key.

5 Position the mouse ⍦ over the program you want to start automatically.

6 Press and hold down the left button as you drag the program to the StartUp folder.

7 To display the contents of the StartUp folder, move the mouse ⍦ over **StartUp** and then quickly press the left button twice.

■ A shortcut to the program appears in the folder.

■ The programs in the StartUp folder start automatically every time you turn on your computer.

ADD AN ITEM TO THE START MENU

You can add your favorite files, folders and programs to the Start menu for quick access.

ADD AN ITEM TO THE START MENU

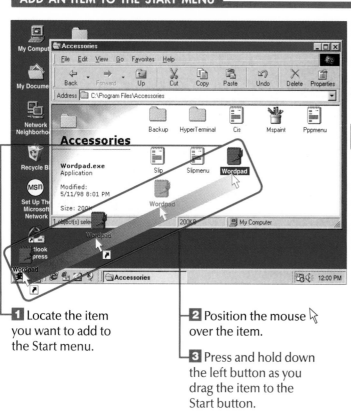

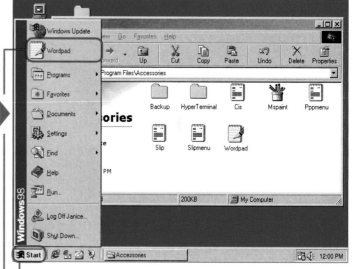

1 Locate the item you want to add to the Start menu.

2 Position the mouse ⌖ over the item.

3 Press and hold down the left button as you drag the item to the Start button.

4 To view the item on the Start menu, move the mouse ⌖ over **Start** and then press the left button.

■ To open the item, move the mouse ⌖ over the item and then press the left button.

■ To close the Start menu without opening the item, move the mouse ⌖ outside the Start menu and then press the left button.

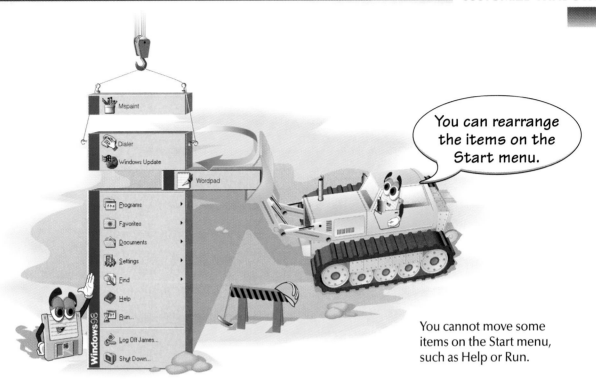

You can rearrange the items on the Start menu.

You cannot move some items on the Start menu, such as Help or Run.

REARRANGE ITEMS ON THE START MENU

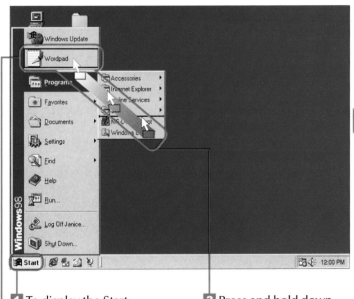

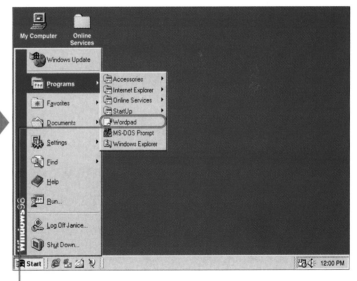

1 To display the Start menu, move the mouse over **Start** and then press the left button.

2 Position the mouse over the item you want to move.

3 Press and hold down the left button as you drag the item to a new location on the Start menu.

Note: A black line indicates where the item will appear.

■ The item appears in the new location.

You can remove an item you no longer want to appear on the Start menu.

You may want to remove a file or program you no longer use.

REMOVE AN ITEM FROM THE START MENU

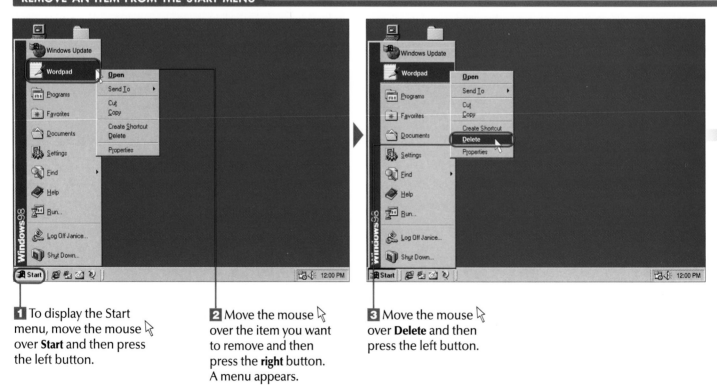

1 To display the Start menu, move the mouse ⟍ over **Start** and then press the left button.

2 Move the mouse ⟍ over the item you want to remove and then press the **right** button. A menu appears.

3 Move the mouse ⟍ over **Delete** and then press the left button.

Does removing an item from the Start menu delete the item from my computer?

Removing a file or program from the Start menu does not delete the item from your computer.

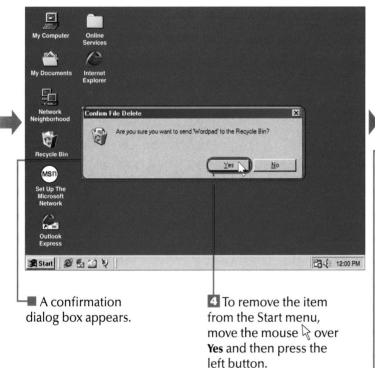

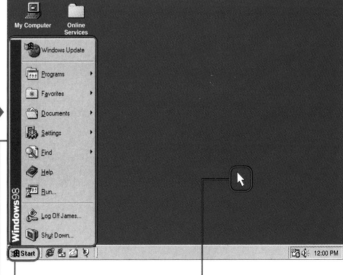

■ A confirmation dialog box appears.

4 To remove the item from the Start menu, move the mouse ⬆ over **Yes** and then press the left button.

5 To confirm that Windows removed the item, move the mouse ⬆ over **Start** and then press the left button.

■ The item no longer appears on the Start menu.

6 To close the Start menu without selecting an item, move the mouse ⬆ outside the Start menu and then press the left button.

If you have difficulty reading the information displayed on the screen, you can use Magnifier to show an enlarged area of the screen.

If the Accessibility menu is not available on the Start menu, you need to add the Accessibility Tools component from the Accessibility category. To add Windows components, see page 94. Adding the Accessibility Tools component will install Magnifier on your computer.

USING MAGNIFIER

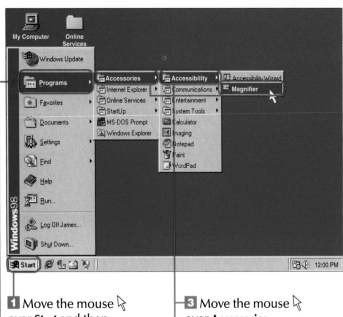

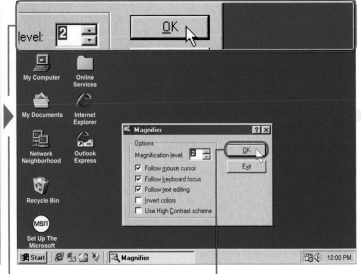

1 Move the mouse ⌖ over **Start** and then press the left button.

2 Move the mouse ⌖ over **Programs**.

3 Move the mouse ⌖ over **Accessories**.

4 Move the mouse ⌖ over **Accessibility**.

5 Move the mouse ⌖ over **Magnifier** and then press the left button.

■ The Magnifier window appears, showing an enlarged view of the screen surrounding the mouse ⌖.

■ The Magnifier dialog box also appears.

6 To reduce the Magnifier dialog box to a button on the taskbar, move the mouse ⌖ over **OK** and then press the left button.

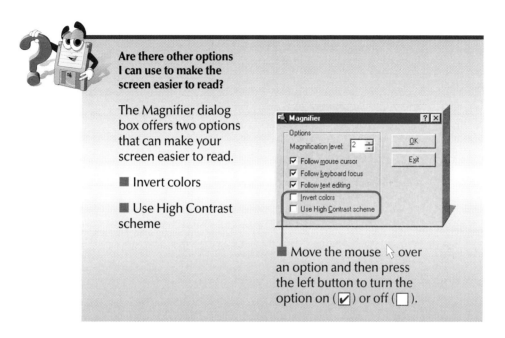

**Are there other options
I can use to make the
screen easier to read?**

The Magnifier dialog
box offers two options
that can make your
screen easier to read.

■ Invert colors

■ Use High Contrast
scheme

■ Move the mouse ⫳ over
an option and then press
the left button to turn the
option on (☑) or off (☐).

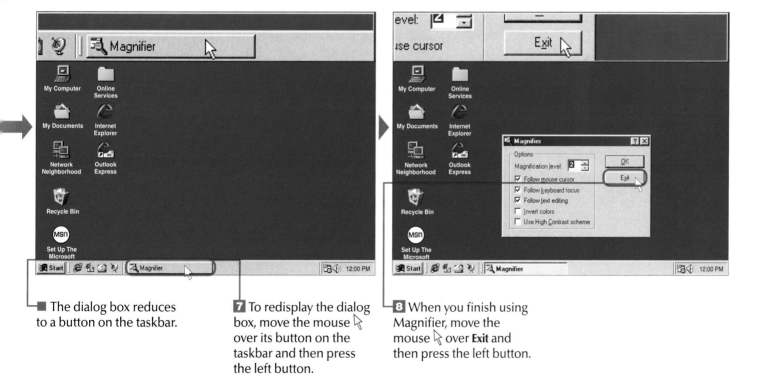

■ The dialog box reduces
to a button on the taskbar.

7 To redisplay the dialog
box, move the mouse ⫳
over its button on the
taskbar and then press
the left button.

8 When you finish using
Magnifier, move the
mouse ⫳ over **Exit** and
then press the left button.

The Accessibility Wizard can help you set up Windows to meet your vision, hearing and mobility needs.

Although the accessibility options are designed for people with special needs, there are some options which may be of interest to all users.

If the Accessibility menu is not available on the Start menu, you need to add the Accessibility Tools component from the Accessibility category. To add Windows components, see page 94.

USING THE ACCESSIBILITY WIZARD

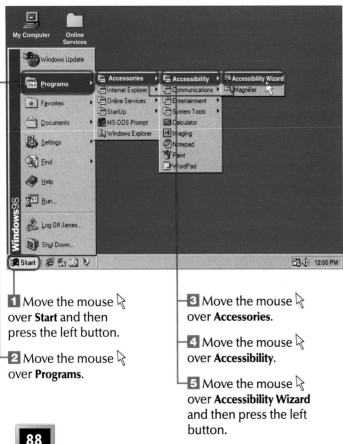

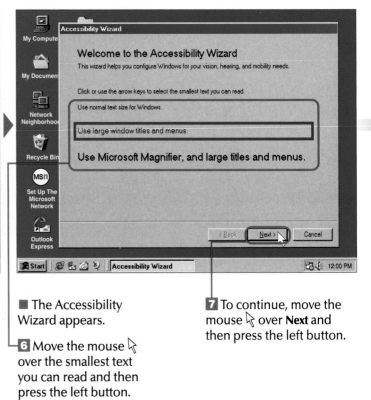

1 Move the mouse over **Start** and then press the left button.

2 Move the mouse over **Programs**.

3 Move the mouse over **Accessories**.

4 Move the mouse over **Accessibility**.

5 Move the mouse over **Accessibility Wizard** and then press the left button.

■ The Accessibility Wizard appears.

6 Move the mouse over the smallest text you can read and then press the left button.

7 To continue, move the mouse over **Next** and then press the left button.

What changes can the Accessibility Wizard make to my computer?

Vision
Make information easier to see by changing the size of items and the colors displayed on the screen.

Hearing
Display visual warnings when events occur and display messages for sounds.

Mobility
Make the keyboard and mouse easier to use.

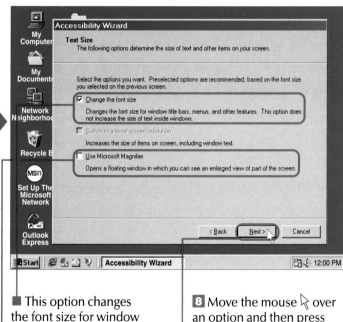

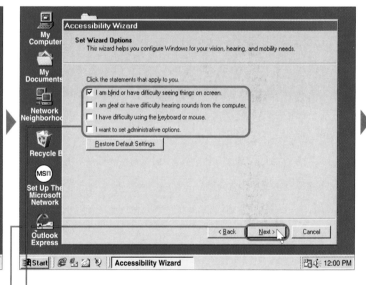

■ This option changes the font size for window title bars, menus and other features.

■ This option magnifies a portion of your screen.

8 Move the mouse ⍺ over an option and then press the left button to turn the option on (☑) or off (☐).

9 To continue, move the mouse ⍺ over **Next** and then press the left button.

10 Move the mouse ⍺ over each statement that applies to you and then press the left button (☐ changes to ☑).

11 To continue, move the mouse ⍺ over **Next** and then press the left button.

■ The options available in the next screens depend on the statement(s) you selected in step 10.

CONTINUED➡

The Accessibility Wizard helps you choose options that will benefit you the most when using Windows.

USING THE ACCESSIBILITY WIZARD (CONTINUED)

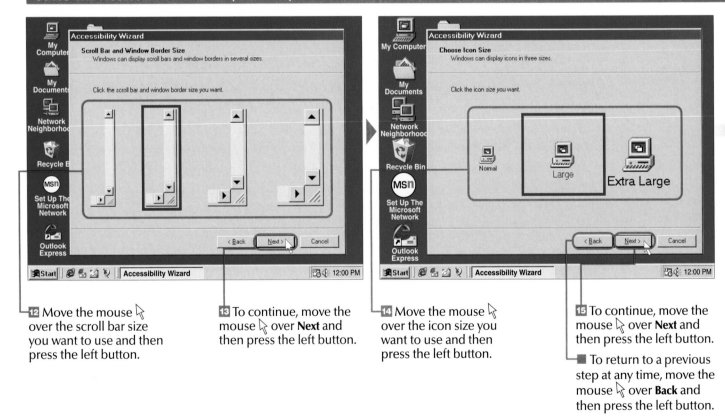

12 Move the mouse ⟨ over the scroll bar size you want to use and then press the left button.

13 To continue, move the mouse ⟨ over **Next** and then press the left button.

14 Move the mouse ⟨ over the icon size you want to use and then press the left button.

15 To continue, move the mouse ⟨ over **Next** and then press the left button.

■ To return to a previous step at any time, move the mouse ⟨ over **Back** and then press the left button.

Where can I find more information to assist users with special needs?

The Microsoft Accessibility and Disabilities Web page contains useful information to assist users with their vision, hearing and mobility needs. You can find this Web page at www.microsoft.com/enable

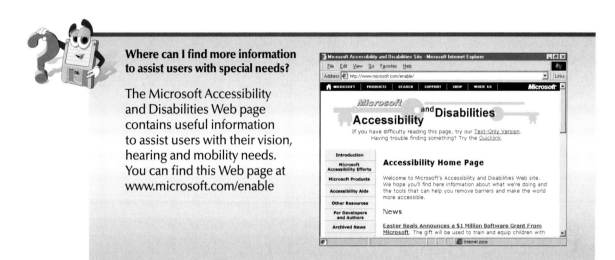

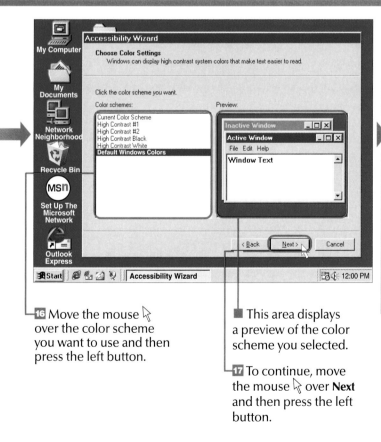

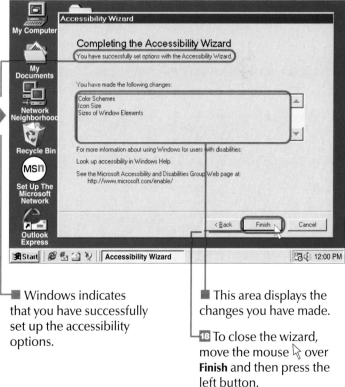

■16 Move the mouse ⬚ over the color scheme you want to use and then press the left button.

■ This area displays a preview of the color scheme you selected.

■17 To continue, move the mouse ⬚ over **Next** and then press the left button.

■ Windows indicates that you have successfully set up the accessibility options.

■ This area displays the changes you have made.

■18 To close the wizard, move the mouse ⬚ over **Finish** and then press the left button.

CHAPTER 5

OPTIMIZE YOUR COMPUTER

Are you interested in improving the performance of your computer? In this chapter you will learn how to add Windows components, install a program, view hardware information and more.

EXTRA **Windows Components**

You can add Windows components to your computer that were not added when you first set up Windows.

When setting up Windows, most people do not install all the components that come with the program. This prevents unneeded components from taking up storage space on the computer.

ADD WINDOWS COMPONENTS

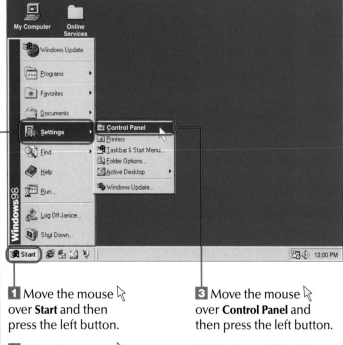

1 Move the mouse ⌖ over **Start** and then press the left button.

2 Move the mouse ⌖ over **Settings**.

3 Move the mouse ⌖ over **Control Panel** and then press the left button.

■ The Control Panel window appears.

4 Move the mouse ⌖ over **Add/Remove Programs** and then quickly press the left button twice.

■ The Add/Remove Programs Properties dialog box appears.

94

Which Windows components can I add to my computer?

Windows components you can add to your computer include:

Accessibility Tools
Sets up Windows to meet vision, hearing and mobility needs.

Backup
Copies important information from your computer to floppy disks or a tape drive. This will protect the information from computer failure or theft.

Web Publishing Wizard
Allows you to publish your own Web pages on the Internet.

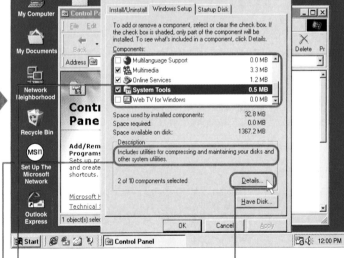

5 Move the mouse ⌖ over the **Windows Setup** tab and then press the left button.

Note: Windows may take a moment to display the information.

■ This area displays the categories of components you can add to your computer.

■ The box beside each category indicates if all (☑), some (☑) or none (☐) of the components in the category are installed on your computer.

6 To display a description of the components in a category, move the mouse ⌖ over the category and then press the left button.

■ This area displays the description.

7 To display the components in the category, move the mouse ⌖ over **Details** and then press the left button.

CONTINUED➡

When adding Windows components, you will be asked to insert the CD-ROM disc you used to install Windows.

ADD WINDOWS COMPONENTS (CONTINUED)

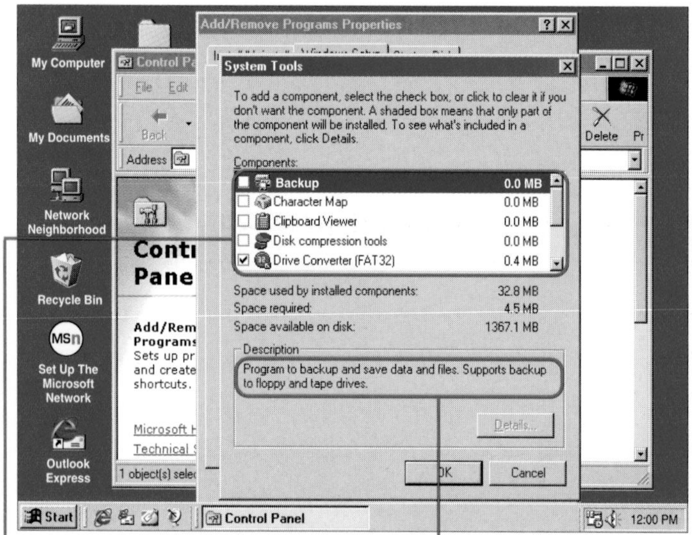
Add/Remove Programs Properties
System Tools
To add a component, select the check box, or click to clear it if you don't want the component. A shaded box means that only part of the component will be installed. To see what's included in a component, click Details.
Components:
Backup 0.0 MB
Character Map 0.0 MB
Clipboard Viewer 0.0 MB
Disk compression tools 0.0 MB
Drive Converter (FAT32) 0.4 MB
Space used by installed components: 32.8 MB
Space required: 4.5 MB
Space available on disk: 1367.1 MB
Description
Program to backup and save data and files. Supports backup to floppy and tape drives.
Details...
OK
Cancel
Control Panel
12:00 PM

■ The components in the category appear. The box beside each component indicates if the component is installed (☑) or not installed (☐) on your computer.

■ This area displays a description of the highlighted component.

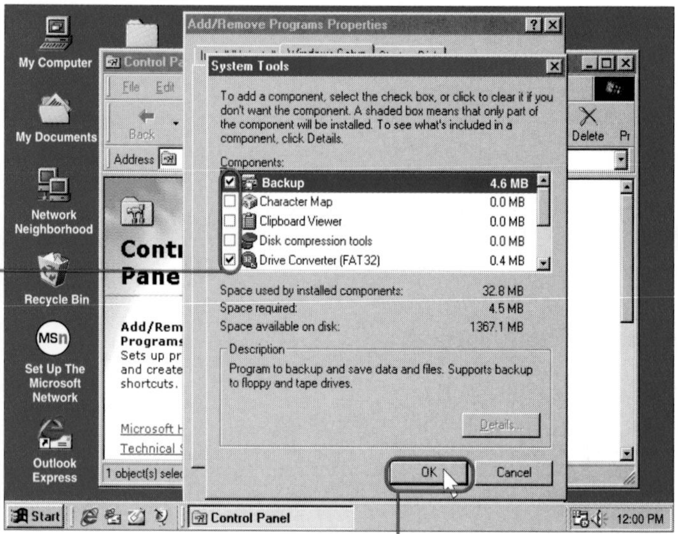
Add/Remove Programs Properties
System Tools
To add a component, select the check box, or click to clear it if you don't want the component. A shaded box means that only part of the component will be installed. To see what's included in a component, click Details.
Components:
Backup 4.6 MB
Character Map 0.0 MB
Clipboard Viewer 0.0 MB
Disk compression tools 0.0 MB
Drive Converter (FAT32) 0.4 MB
Space used by installed components: 32.8 MB
Space required: 4.5 MB
Space available on disk: 1367.1 MB
Description
Program to backup and save data and files. Supports backup to floppy and tape drives.
Details...
OK
Cancel
Control Panel
12:00 PM

8 Move the mouse ↖ over the box (☐) beside the component you want to add to your computer and then press the left button (☐ changes to ☑).

9 To confirm your change, move the mouse ↖ over **OK** and then press the left button.

How do I remove a Windows component I do not use?

You can remove a Windows component you do not use to free up space on your computer. To remove a Windows component, perform steps 1 to 10 starting on page 94. When you select a Windows component you want to remove, ☑ changes to ☐ in step 8.

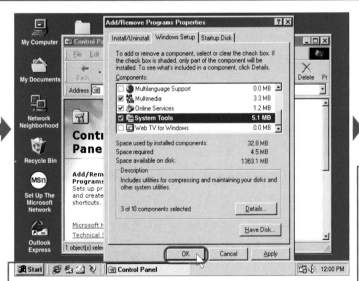

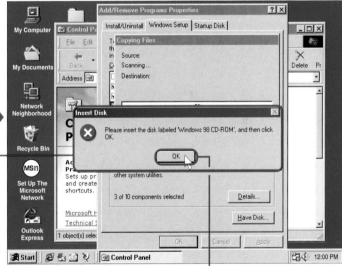

◾ 10 To close the Add/Remove Programs Properties dialog box, move the mouse ⇖ over **OK** and then press the left button.

◾ The Insert Disk dialog box appears, asking you to insert the Windows 98 CD-ROM disc.

◾ 11 Insert the CD-ROM disc into the drive.

◾ 12 To continue, move the mouse ⇖ over **OK** and then press the left button.

◾ Windows copies the necessary files to your computer.

Note: Windows may ask you to restart your computer.

You can add a new program to your computer. Programs come on a CD-ROM disc or floppy disks.

After you install a program, make sure you keep the program's CD-ROM disc or floppy disks in a safe place. If your computer fails or you accidentally erase the program files, you may need to install the program again.

INSTALL A PROGRAM

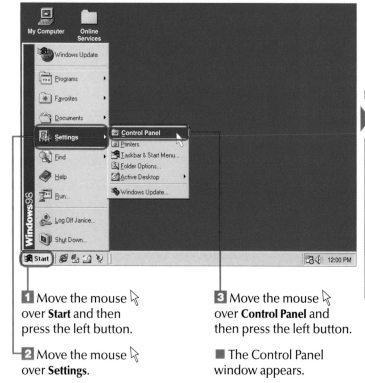

1 Move the mouse over **Start** and then press the left button.

2 Move the mouse over **Settings**.

3 Move the mouse over **Control Panel** and then press the left button.

■ The Control Panel window appears.

4 Move the mouse over **Add/Remove Programs** and then quickly press the left button twice.

■ The Add/Remove Programs Properties dialog box appears.

Why did an installation program start automatically?

Most Windows programs available on a CD-ROM disc will automatically start an installation program when you insert the CD-ROM disc into the drive. Follow the instructions on your screen to install the program.

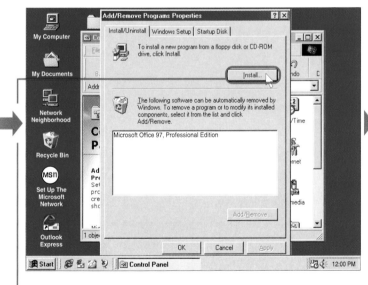

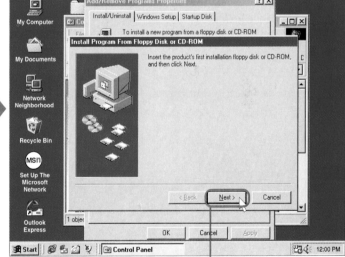

5 To install a new program, move the mouse ⌖ over **Install** and then press the left button.

■ The Install Program From Floppy Disk or CD-ROM wizard appears.

6 Insert the program's first installation floppy disk or CD-ROM disc into a drive.

7 To continue, move the mouse ⌖ over **Next** and then press the left button.

CONTINUED➡

There are three common ways to install a program.

Typical
Sets up the program with the most common components.

Custom
Lets you customize the program to suit your needs.

Minimum
Sets up the minimum amount of the program needed. This is ideal for computers with limited disk space.

INSTALL A PROGRAM (CONTINUED)

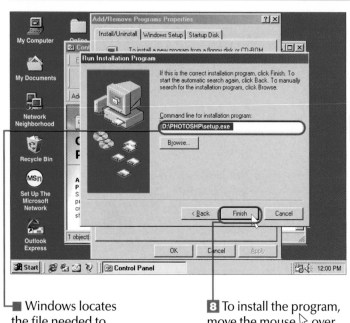

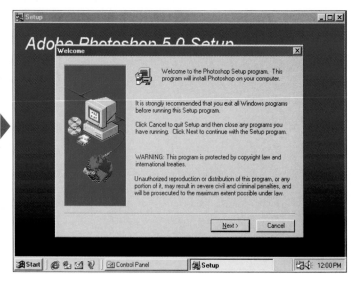

■ Windows locates the file needed to install the program.

8 To install the program, move the mouse ⟋ over **Finish** and then press the left button.

9 Follow the instructions on your screen. Every program will ask you a different set of questions.

You can remove a program you no longer use from your computer. Removing a program will free up space on your hard drive.

REMOVE A PROGRAM

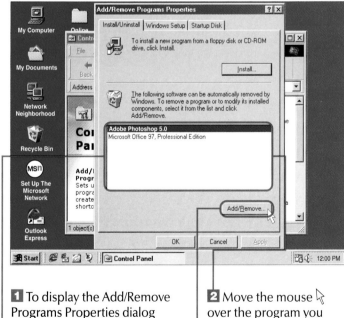

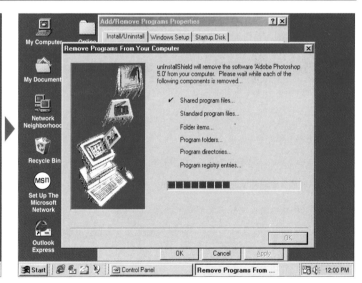

1 To display the Add/Remove Programs Properties dialog box, perform steps 1 to 4 on page 98.

■ This area lists the programs Windows can automatically remove.

2 Move the mouse ⬚ over the program you want to remove and then press the left button.

3 Move the mouse ⬚ over **Add/Remove** and then press the left button.

4 Follow the instructions on your screen. Every program will take you through different steps to remove the program.

You can use the Device Manager to view a list of the hardware devices installed on your computer.

The Device Manager organizes hardware devices into categories, such as disk drives and monitors.

VIEW HARDWARE INFORMATION

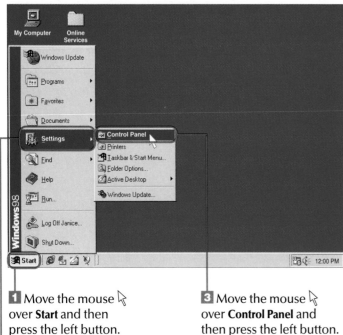

1 Move the mouse over **Start** and then press the left button.

2 Move the mouse over **Settings**.

3 Move the mouse over **Control Panel** and then press the left button.

■ The Control Panel window appears.

4 Move the mouse over **System** and then quickly press the left button twice.

■ The System Properties dialog box appears.

Can the Device Manager help identify problems with my computer hardware?

A hardware device icon with an X indicates the device has been disabled.

A hardware device icon with an exclamation mark (!) indicates the device has a problem.

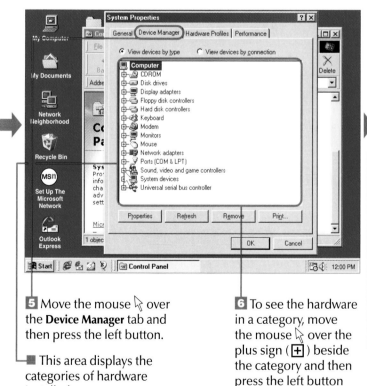

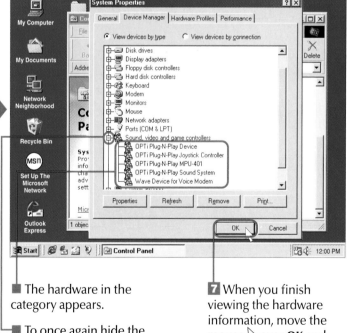

5 Move the mouse ⌖ over the **Device Manager** tab and then press the left button.

■ This area displays the categories of hardware installed on your computer.

6 To see the hardware in a category, move the mouse ⌖ over the plus sign (⊞) beside the category and then press the left button (⊞ changes to ⊟).

■ The hardware in the category appears.

■ To once again hide the hardware in the category, move the mouse ⌖ over the minus sign (⊟) beside the category and then press the left button.

7 When you finish viewing the hardware information, move the mouse ⌖ over **OK** and then press the left button to close the dialog box.

You can have Windows detect and install new hardware for you.

You can add hardware such as a mouse, keyboard or modem.

INSTALL NEW HARDWARE

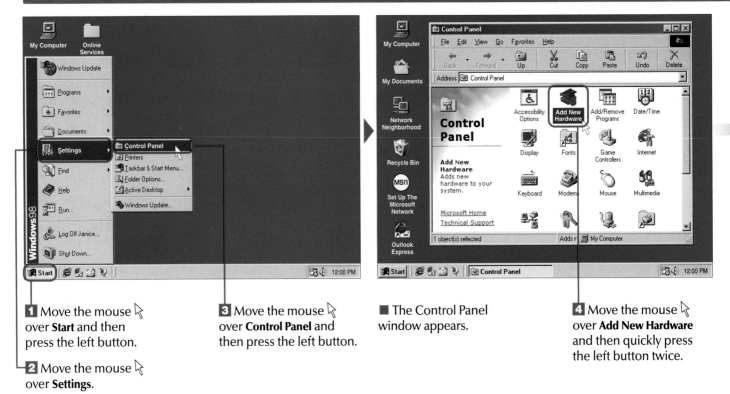

1 Move the mouse over **Start** and then press the left button.

2 Move the mouse over **Settings**.

3 Move the mouse over **Control Panel** and then press the left button.

■ The Control Panel window appears.

4 Move the mouse over **Add New Hardware** and then quickly press the left button twice.

What are Plug and Play devices?

Plug and Play devices are devices that Windows can automatically set up to work properly with your computer, which makes them easy to install. When purchasing a new device for your computer, you should try to purchase a Plug and Play device.

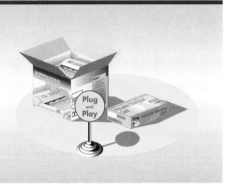

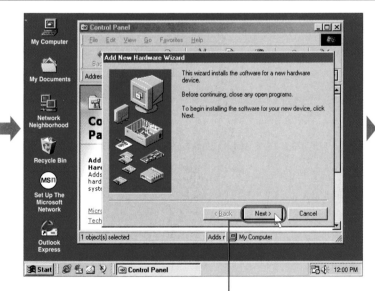

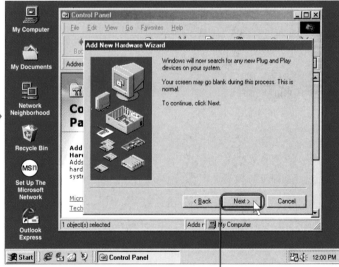

■ The Add New Hardware Wizard appears.

■ Windows tells you to close any open programs before continuing.

5 To begin installing the new hardware, move the mouse ⌖ over **Next** and then press the left button.

■ The wizard informs you that Windows will search for any new Plug and Play devices on your computer.

6 To start the search, move the mouse ⌖ over **Next** and then press the left button.

CONTINUED➡

The wizard guides you step-by-step through the installation, first detecting the hardware and then installing the software needed by the hardware.

INSTALL NEW HARDWARE (CONTINUED)

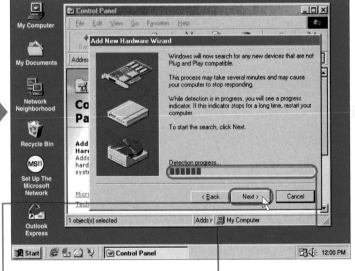

■ Windows will also search for hardware you added to your computer that is not Plug and Play.

7 To have Windows search for hardware that is not Plug and Play, move the mouse ⟲ over **Yes** and then press the left button (○ changes to ⊙).

8 To continue, move the mouse ⟲ over **Next** and then press the left button.

■ Windows is ready to search for new hardware that is not Plug and Play.

9 To start the search, move the mouse ⟲ over **Next** and then press the left button.

■ This area displays the progress of the search. The search may take several minutes.

*Note: To stop the search, move the mouse ⟲ over **Cancel** and then press the left button.*

Is there hardware I can install that will make typing more comfortable?

You may want to purchase and install an ergonomically designed keyboard. Ergonomically designed keyboards position your hands naturally and support your wrists so you can work more comfortably at your computer.

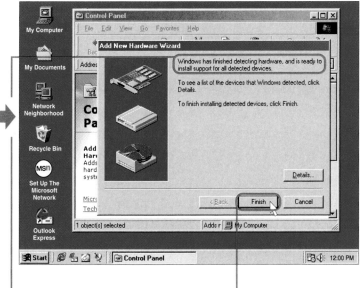

■ This message appears when Windows has finished searching for the new hardware.

10 To finish installing the new hardware, move the mouse over **Finish** and then press the left button.

■ This area describes the hardware Windows found.

11 To continue, move the mouse over **Next** and then press the left button.

■ You may be asked to insert the Windows CD-ROM disc and restart your computer.

■ You can now use your new hardware.

You can use Windows Update to find software that can enhance and optimize the performance of your computer.

USING WINDOWS UPDATE

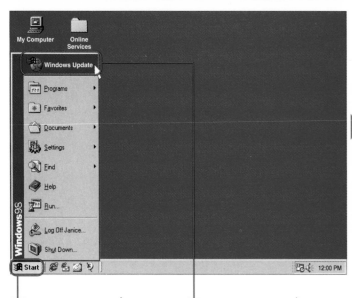

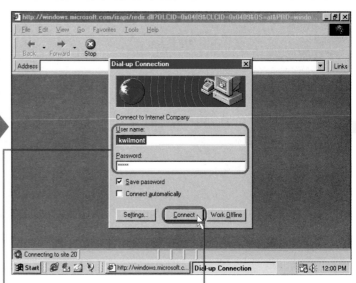

1 Move the mouse ▷ over **Start** and then press the left button.

2 Move the mouse ▷ over **Windows Update** and then press the left button.

■ If you are not connected to the Internet, the Dial-up Connection dialog box appears.

■ This area displays your user name and password.

Note: A symbol (x) appears for each character in your password to prevent others from viewing the password.

3 To connect to your Internet service provider, move the mouse ▷ over **Connect** and then press the left button.

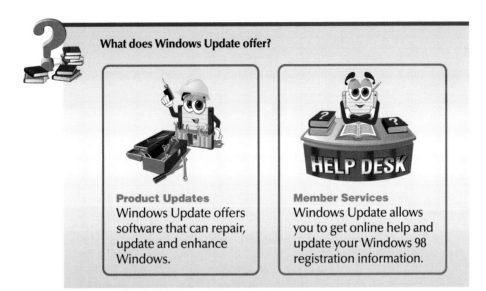

What does Windows Update offer?

Product Updates
Windows Update offers software that can repair, update and enhance Windows.

Member Services
Windows Update allows you to get online help and update your Windows 98 registration information.

■ The Microsoft Windows Update Web page appears. You can use the Web page to update Windows.

Note: The Web page shown on your screen may look different than the Web page shown here. Companies often change their Web pages to add new information and enhance the appearance of the pages.

◄ To view software that can optimize and enhance your computer, move the mouse over **Product Updates** and then press the left button. Then follow the instructions on your screen.

You can optimize your computer by converting your hard drive to the FAT32 file system.

Converting your hard drive to FAT32 will give you additional hard drive space and allow your programs to start faster.

CONVERT YOUR DRIVE TO FAT32

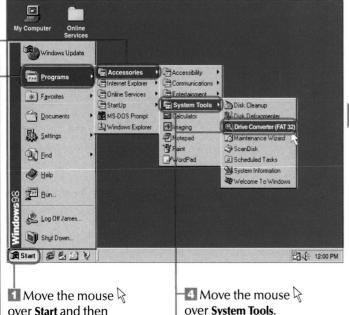

1 Move the mouse over **Start** and then press the left button.

2 Move the mouse over **Programs**.

3 Move the mouse over **Accessories**.

4 Move the mouse over **System Tools**.

5 Move the mouse over **Drive Converter (FAT32)** and then press the left button.

■ The Drive Converter (FAT32) wizard appears.

■ This area provides information about the wizard.

6 To continue, move the mouse over **Next** and then press the left button.

How does converting to FAT32 give me additional hard drive space?

Your hard drive stores data in groups called clusters. Windows uses the File Allocation Table (FAT) to keep track of which clusters store the files on your hard drive. The FAT32 file system stores data in smaller clusters than the older FAT system. This reduces wasted space on your hard drive, which provides additional storage space.

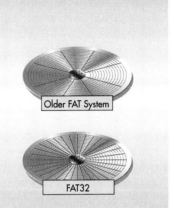

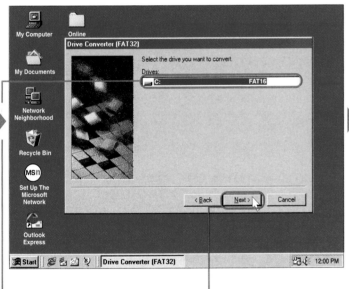

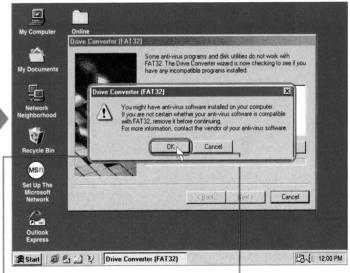

7 Move the mouse ▷ over the drive you want to convert to FAT32 and then press the left button.

8 To continue, move the mouse ▷ over **Next** and then press the left button.

■ A warning message appears, asking you to remove any anti-virus software that will not work with FAT32 from your computer.

Note: If you are not sure if you should remove a program, you can contact the manufacturer of the program.

9 To continue, move the mouse ▷ over **OK** and then press the left button.

CONTINUED➡

Before converting your drive, the wizard will search your computer for anti-virus and disk utility programs that do not work with FAT32.

Anti-virus program
Detects and removes viruses to prevent computer problems.

Disk utility program
Optimizes your computer for better performance.

CONVERT YOUR DRIVE TO FAT32 (CONTINUED)

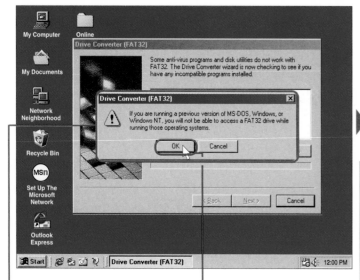

■ A second warning message appears, stating that you will not be able to access a FAT32 drive while running a previous version of MS-DOS, Windows or Windows NT.

Note: A computer can be set up to run more than one operating system.

10 To continue, move the mouse ⊳ over **OK** and then press the left button.

■ The wizard searches for anti-virus and disk utility programs that do not work with FAT32.

■ This message appears if Windows did not find any programs that do not work with FAT32.

11 To continue, move the mouse ⊳ over **Next** and then press the left button.

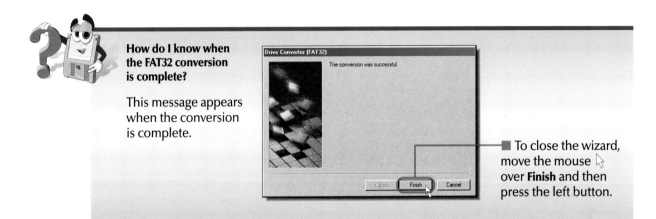

How do I know when the FAT32 conversion is complete?

This message appears when the conversion is complete.

■ To close the wizard, move the mouse ▷ over **Finish** and then press the left button.

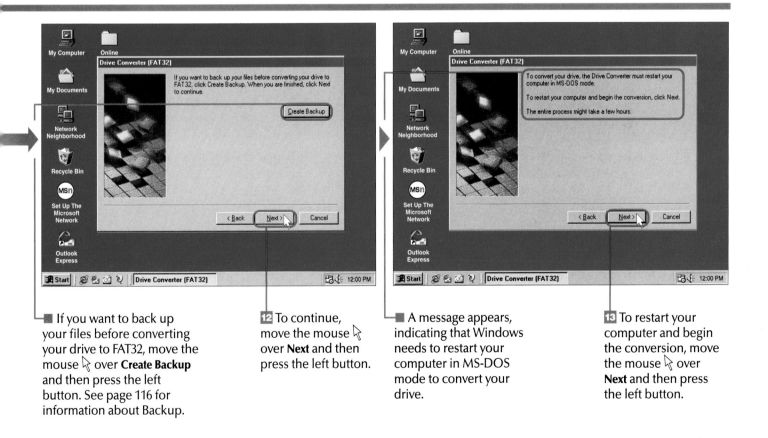

■ If you want to back up your files before converting your drive to FAT32, move the mouse ▷ over **Create Backup** and then press the left button. See page 116 for information about Backup.

12 To continue, move the mouse ▷ over **Next** and then press the left button.

■ A message appears, indicating that Windows needs to restart your computer in MS-DOS mode to convert your drive.

13 To restart your computer and begin the conversion, move the mouse ▷ over **Next** and then press the left button.

CHAPTER 6

BACK UP FILES

Are you wondering how to protect important information stored on your computer? This chapter shows you how to back up your files.

You can make backup copies of important information stored on your computer. This will protect the data from theft, fire, viruses and computer failure.

If the Backup feature is not available, you need to add the Backup component from the System Tools category. To add Windows components, see page 94.

BACK UP FILES

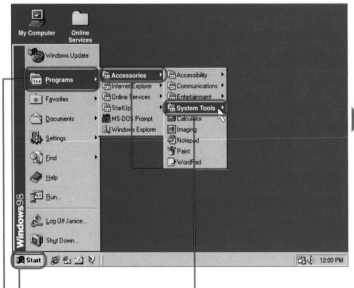

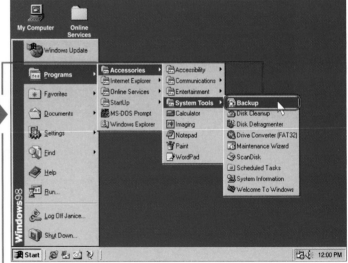

1 Move the mouse over **Start** and then press the left button.

2 Move the mouse over **Programs**.

3 Move the mouse over **Accessories**.

4 Move the mouse over **System Tools**.

5 Move the mouse over **Backup** and then press the left button.

*Note: A dialog box appears if Windows does not find any backup devices on your computer. If you are using a tape drive, move the mouse over **Yes** and then press the left button to install the drive. If you are not using a tape drive as your backup device, select **No**.*

What devices can I use to back up my information?

You can use many types of devices to back up your information, including a floppy drive, second hard drive, removable drive, network drive or tape drive. Most people perform backups using a tape drive since this type of device is inexpensive and can back up a large amount of information.

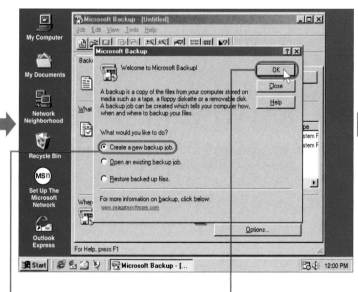

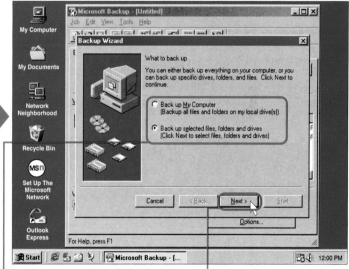

■ The Microsoft Backup window and dialog box appear.

6 Move the mouse ⓀΔ over **Create a new backup job** and then press the left button (○ changes to ⊙).

7 To continue, move the mouse ⓀΔ over **OK** and then press the left button.

8 Move the mouse ⓀΔ over an option to back up everything on your computer or just specific files, folders and drives and then press the left button (○ changes to ⊙).

9 To continue, move the mouse ⓀΔ over **Next** and then press the left button.

*Note: If you selected **Back up My Computer** in step 8, skip to step 15 on page 120.*

CONT☺NUED➡

You must select which files and folders you want to back up on your computer.

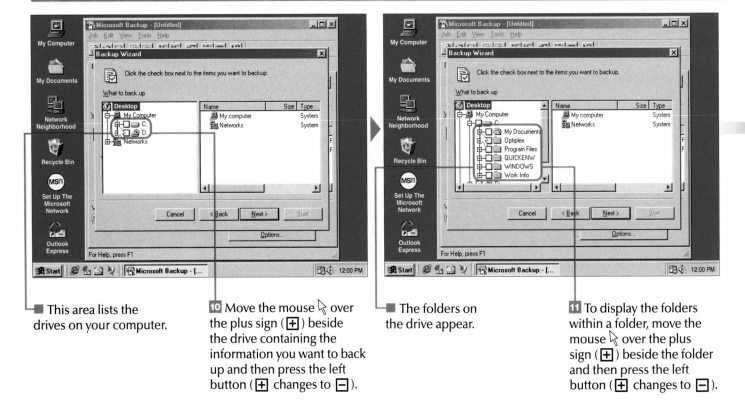

■ This area lists the drives on your computer.

10 Move the mouse ⌖ over the plus sign (⊞) beside the drive containing the information you want to back up and then press the left button (⊞ changes to ⊟).

■ The folders on the drive appear.

11 To display the folders within a folder, move the mouse ⌖ over the plus sign (⊞) beside the folder and then press the left button (⊞ changes to ⊟).

Can I use Backup to perform other tasks?

Archive Data
You can use Backup to copy old or rarely used files from your computer to tape cartridges. You can then remove the files from your computer to free up storage space.

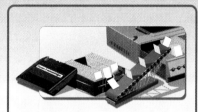

Transfer Data
You can use Backup to copy information from your computer to tape cartridges. You can then transfer the files to another computer.

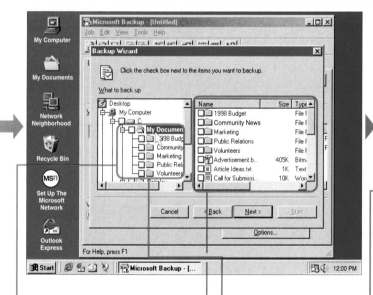

■ The folders appear.

■ To hide the folders, move the mouse ⌖ over the minus sign (⊟) beside the folder and then press the left button.

12 To display the contents of a folder, move the mouse ⌖ over the folder and then press the left button.

■ This area displays the contents of the folder.

13 Move the mouse ⌖ over the box (☐) beside each item you want to back up and then press the left button (☐ changes to ☑).

■ The box beside each drive or folder indicates if all (☑), some (☑) or none (☐) of the items it contains are selected.

14 To continue, move the mouse ⌖ over **Next** and then press the left button.

CONTINUED

You can back up all the files you selected or only the files that are new or have changed since a previous backup.

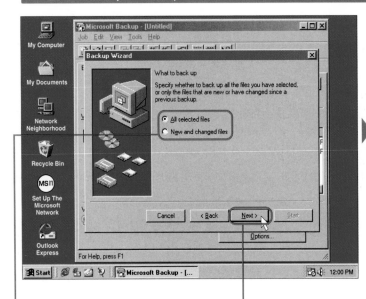

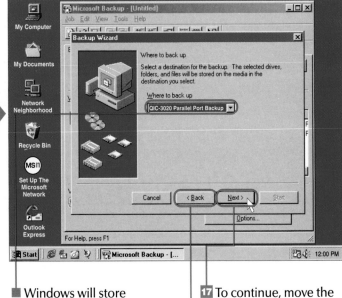

15 Move the mouse ⬦ over an option to back up all the files you selected or only the files that are new or have changed since a previous backup and then press the left button (○ changes to ⊙).

16 To continue, move the mouse ⬦ over **Next** and then press the left button.

■ Windows will store the backup in the location shown in this area.

17 To continue, move the mouse ⬦ over **Next** and then press the left button.

■ To return to a previous step at any time, move the mouse ⬦ over **Back** and then press the left button.

How often should I back up my information?

To determine how often you should back up your information, consider how much work you can afford to lose. If you cannot afford to lose the work accomplished in one day, back up your files once a day. If your work does not often change during the week, back up once a week.

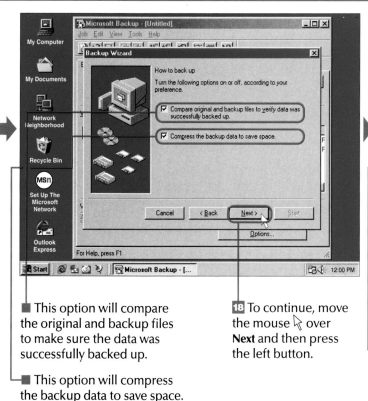

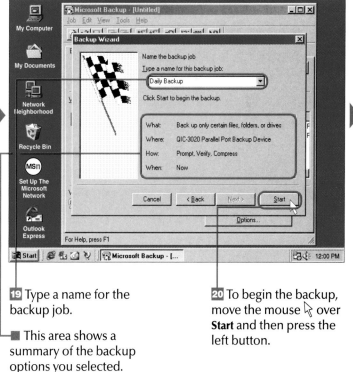

■ This option will compare the original and backup files to make sure the data was successfully backed up.

■ This option will compress the backup data to save space.

18 To continue, move the mouse ☈ over **Next** and then press the left button.

19 Type a name for the backup job.

■ This area shows a summary of the backup options you selected.

20 To begin the backup, move the mouse ☈ over **Start** and then press the left button.

CONTINUED➡

When the backup is complete, store the backup copies in a cool, dry place, away from electrical equipment and magnetic devices.

BACK UP FILES (CONTINUED)

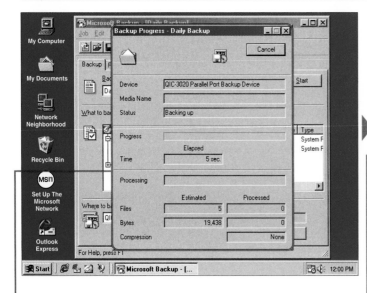

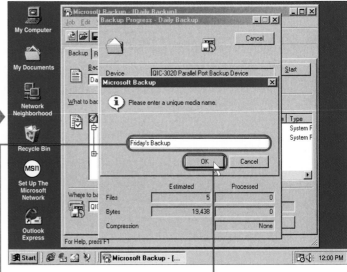

■ The Backup Progress window appears, showing you the progress of the backup.

■ A dialog box may appear, asking you to enter a unique name for the tape.

21 Type a name for the tape.

22 To continue, move the mouse � over **OK** and then press the left button.

Why does this dialog box appear when I perform a backup?

This dialog box appears if the tape cartridge you are using already contains a backup. Move the mouse ⌖ over the option you want to use and then press the left button.

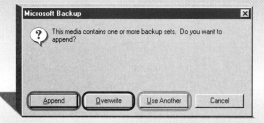

Use Another
Allows you to use another tape.

Append
Adds the current backup without replacing the existing backup.

Overwrite
Replaces the existing backup with the current backup.

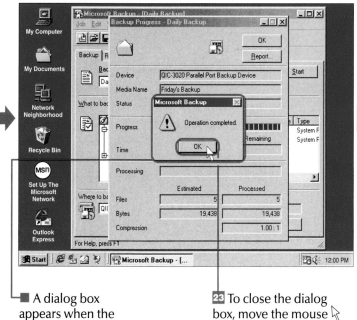

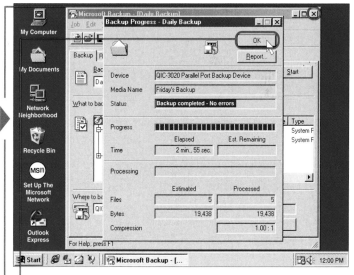

■ A dialog box appears when the backup is complete.

23 To close the dialog box, move the mouse ⌖ over **OK** and then press the left button.

24 To close the Backup Progress window, move the mouse ⌖ over **OK** and then press the left button.

25 To close the Microsoft Backup window, move the mouse ⌖ over ⊠ and then press the left button.

Note: You only have to create a backup job once. The next time you want to back up the same files, use the existing backup job. See page 124.

You can open an existing backup job to perform another backup using the same settings.

A backup job contains all the settings for a backup, such as the information to be backed up and where to store the information. To create a backup job, perform the steps starting on page 116.

OPEN AN EXISTING BACKUP JOB

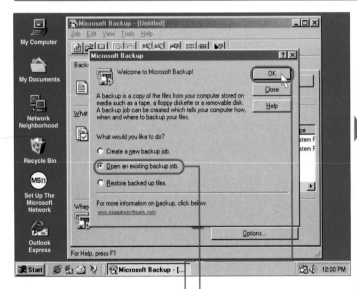

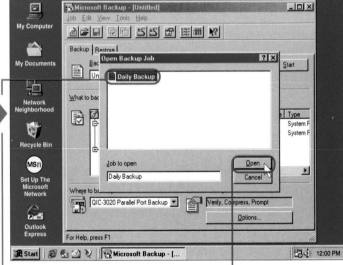

1 To start Microsoft Backup, perform steps 1 to 5 on page 116.

■ The Microsoft Backup window and dialog box appear.

2 Move the mouse ⌖ over **Open an existing backup job** and then press the left button (○ changes to ⊙).

3 To continue, move the mouse ⌖ over **OK** and then press the left button.

■ The Open Backup Job dialog box appears.

4 Move the mouse ⌖ over the backup job you want to open and then press the left button.

5 Move the mouse ⌖ over **Open** and then press the left button.

Can I have more than one backup job?

You can have many backup jobs. For example, you may have one backup job to back up all of your documents at the end of each week. You may have another backup job to back up all of your program files once a month.

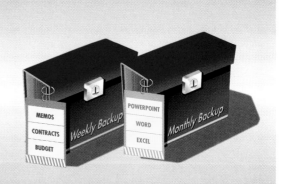

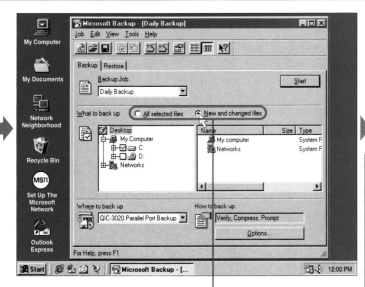

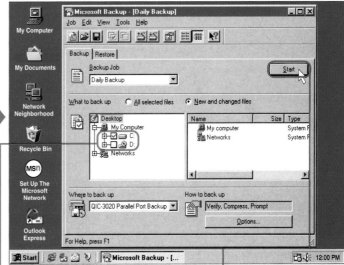

■ Information for the backup job appears in the Microsoft Backup window.

6 Move the mouse ⌖ over an option to back up all the files in the backup job or only the files that are new or have changed since a previous backup and then press the left button (○ changes to ⊙).

■ Windows will back up information on each drive in this area that displays a check mark (☑).

Note: To change which folders and files you want to back up, perform steps 10 to 13 on page 118.

7 Move the mouse ⌖ over **Start** and then press the left button.

■ To complete the backup, perform steps 21 to 25 on page 122.

If files on your computer are lost or damaged, you can use Backup to restore the files.

RESTORE FILES

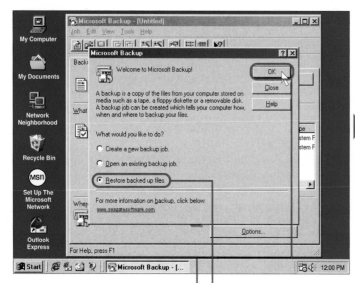

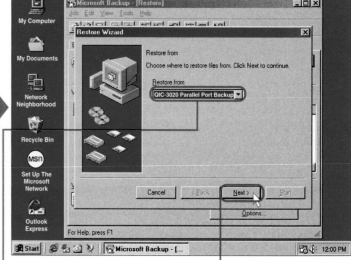

1 Insert the tape containing the information you want to restore into the drive.

2 To start Microsoft Backup, perform steps **1** to **5** on page 116.

■ The Microsoft Backup window and dialog box appear.

3 Move the mouse ⌖ over **Restore backed up files** and then press the left button (○ changes to ⊙).

4 To continue, move the mouse ⌖ over **OK** and then press the left button.

■ The Restore Wizard appears.

■ This area displays the location you will restore the files from.

5 To continue, move the mouse ⌖ over **Next** and then press the left button.

Can I restore just one file?

Yes. You do not have to restore all the files you backed up. You can select only the files you want to restore. This is ideal if you accidentally deleted or made changes to an important file on your computer.

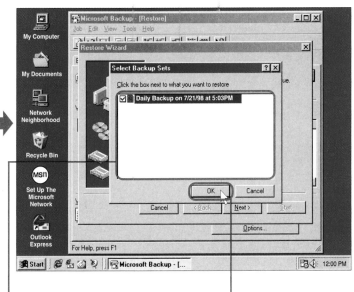

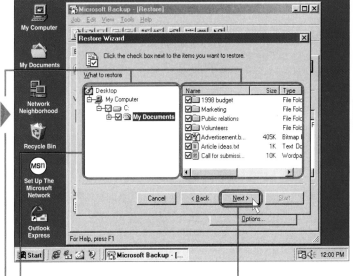

■ Windows will restore each backup job in this area that displays a check mark (☑).

6 To remove a check mark, move the mouse ⇖ over the box beside a backup job and then press the left button (☑ changes to ☐).

7 To continue, move the mouse ⇖ over **OK** and then press the left button.

■ This area displays the drives and folders in the backup job.

Note: To display the contents of a drive or folder, perform steps 10 to 12 on page 118.

8 To select each item you want to restore, move the mouse ⇖ over the box beside each item and then press the left button (☐ changes to ☑).

9 To continue, move the mouse ⇖ over **Next** and then press the left button.

CONTINUED

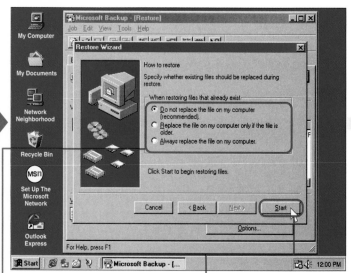

■ Windows will restore the files to the original location on your computer.

10 To continue, move the mouse over **Next** and then press the left button.

■ To return to a previous step at any time, move the mouse over **Back** and then press the left button.

11 To specify how you want to replace existing files on your computer, move the mouse over an option and then press the left button (○ changes to ⊙).

Note: For more information, see the top of page 129.

12 To start the restore, move the mouse over **Start** and then press the left button.

When restoring files, will Backup replace existing files on my computer?

Backup offers you three choices when restoring files.

Do not replace files on your computer.

Replace files on your computer only if the files are older.

Always replace files on your computer.

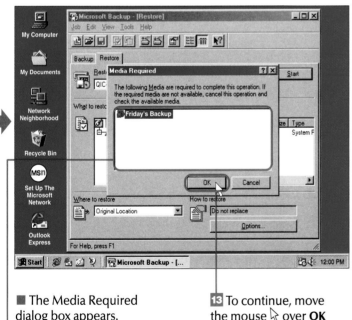

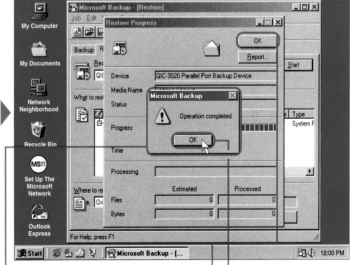

■ The Media Required dialog box appears.

■ This area lists the tapes you will need to restore the files.

13 To continue, move the mouse ⌖ over **OK** and then press the left button.

■ The Restore Progress window appears, showing the progress of the restore.

■ A dialog box appears when the restore is complete.

14 To close the dialog box, move the mouse ⌖ over **OK** and then press the left button.

15 To close the Restore Progress window, move the mouse ⌖ over **OK** and then press the left button.

CHAPTER 7

WORK ON A NETWORK

Would you like to share information and equipment with other computers on a network? Read this chapter to find out how.

A network is a group of connected computers that allow people to share information and equipment.

Before networks, people used floppy disks to exchange information between computers. This method of exchanging information is known as sneakernet. Computer networks eliminate the need for sneakernet.

Share Information

Networks let you easily share data and programs. You can exchange documents, spreadsheets, pictures and electronic mail between computers.

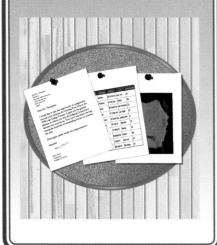

Share Equipment

Computers connected to a network can share equipment, such as a printer, to reduce costs. For example, rather than buying a printer for each person on a network, everyone can share one central printer.

Workgroups

Each computer on a network belongs to a workgroup. Small companies usually have one workgroup. Large companies have many workgroups to better organize information and resources.

Before you can share information or a printer with individuals on a network, you must set up your computer to share resources.

TURN ON SHARING

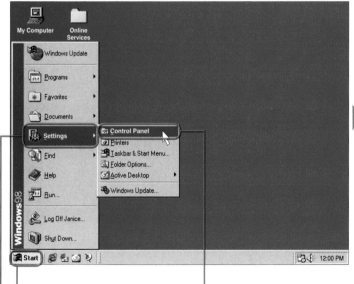

1 Move the mouse over **Start** and then press the left button.

2 Move the mouse over **Settings**.

3 Move the mouse over **Control Panel** and then press the left button.

■ The Control Panel window appears.

4 Move the mouse over **Network** and then quickly press the left button twice.

■ The Network dialog box appears.

CONTINUED➡

Windows requires you to restart your computer before the new sharing settings will take effect.

Make sure you close any open programs before restarting your computer.

TURN ON SHARING (CONTINUED)

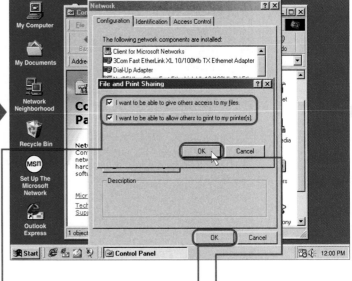

5 Move the mouse ⌖ over **File and Print Sharing** and then press the left button.

■ The File and Print Sharing dialog box appears.

6 If you want to be able to share your files or printer, move the mouse ⌖ over each option you want to use and then press the left button (☐ changes to ☑).

7 Move the mouse ⌖ over **OK** and then press the left button.

8 To close the Network dialog box, move the mouse ⌖ over **OK** and then press the left button.

I turned on sharing, but my colleagues still cannot access my files and printer. What is wrong?

Once you set up your computer to share information or a printer, you must specify exactly what you want to share. To specify the information you want to share, see page 136. To specify the printer you want to share, see page 140.

■ The Insert Disk dialog box appears, asking you to insert the Windows 98 CD-ROM disc.

9 Insert the disc into your CD-ROM drive.

10 To continue, move the mouse ⃝ over **OK** and then press the left button.

■ Windows copies the necessary files to your computer.

■ The System Settings Change dialog box appears, indicating that Windows needs to restart your computer before the new settings will take effect.

11 To restart your computer, move the mouse ⃝ over **Yes** and then press the left button.

■ To turn off file and printer sharing, repeat steps **1** to **11** starting on page 133 (☑ changes to ☐ in step **6**).

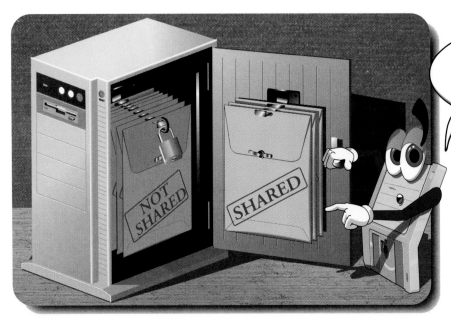

You can specify exactly what information you want to share with individuals on a network.

You must turn on sharing before you can share information. To turn on sharing, see page 133.

SHARE INFORMATION

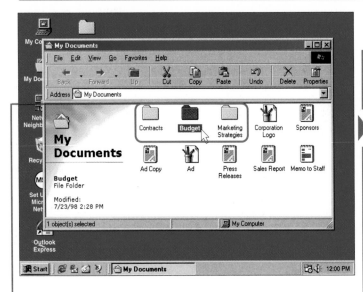

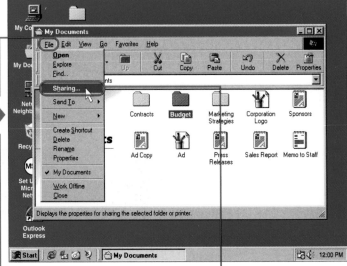

1 Move the mouse over the folder you want to share and then press the left button.

2 Move the mouse over **File** and then press the left button.

3 Move the mouse over **Sharing** and then press the left button.

■ The Properties dialog box appears.

How can I stop sharing a folder?

To stop sharing a folder, repeat steps 1 to 4 starting on page 136, selecting **Not Shared** in step 4. Then move the mouse ⍺ over **OK** in the Properties dialog box and press the left button.

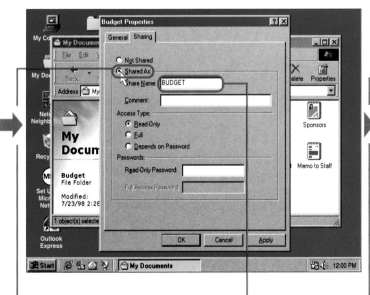

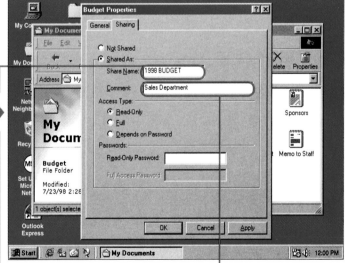

4 To share the folder with others on a network, move the mouse ⍺ over **Shared As:** and then press the left button (○ changes to ⊙).

■ This area displays the name of the folder individuals will see on the network.

5 If you want to give the folder a different name, press and hold down the left button as you drag the mouse I over this area until the text is highlighted. Then type a new name.

6 To enter a comment about the folder, move the mouse I over this area and then press the left button. Then type the comment.

CONTINUED▶

You can assign one of three types of access to the information you share on a network.

SHARE INFORMATION (CONTINUED)

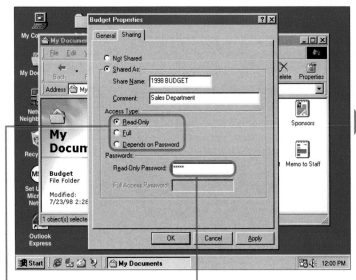

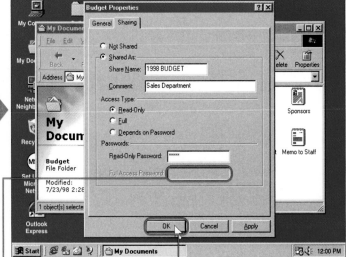

7 Move the mouse ↖ over the type of access you want to assign to the folder and then press the left button (○ changes to ⊙).

8 If you selected Read-Only access and want to assign a password, move the mouse ↖ over this area and then press the left button. Then type a password.

Note: A password prevents unauthorized people from accessing the folder.

9 If you selected Full access and want to assign a password, move the mouse ↖ over this area and then press the left button. Then type a password.

■ If you selected Depends on Password access, perform steps 8 and 9 to enter the passwords you want to use.

10 To confirm your changes, move the mouse ↖ over **OK** and then press the left button.

Read-Only
Individuals on the network can read but cannot change or delete information.

Full
Individuals on the network can read, change and delete information.

Depends on Password
Some individuals on the network have Read-Only access, while others have Full access, depending on which password they enter.

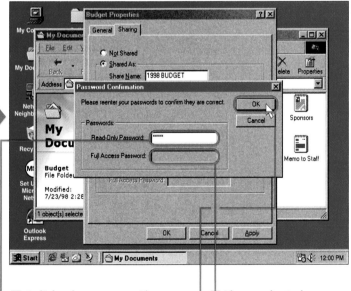

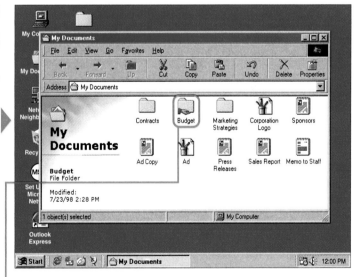

■ A dialog box appears if you entered a password.

11 Retype the password to confirm the password.

■ If you selected Depends on Password access, press the Tab key and then retype the Full Access password.

12 Move the mouse ⌖ over **OK** and then press the left button.

■ A hand appears under the icon for the shared folder.

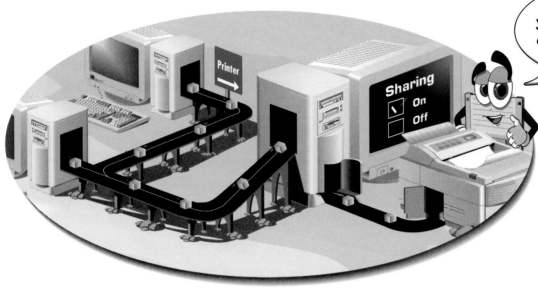

You can share your printer with other individuals on a network.

To share your printer, the printer must be directly connected to your computer and sharing must be turned on. To turn on sharing, see page 133.

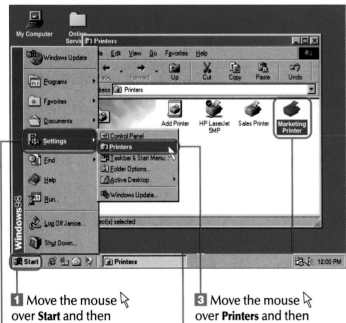

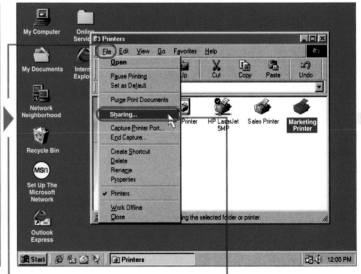

1 Move the mouse ⟋ over **Start** and then press the left button.

2 Move the mouse ⟋ over **Settings**.

3 Move the mouse ⟋ over **Printers** and then press the left button.

■ The Printers window appears.

4 Move the mouse ⟋ over the printer you want to share and then press the left button.

5 Move the mouse ⟋ over **File** and then press the left button.

6 Move the mouse ⟋ over **Sharing** and then press the left button.

■ The Properties dialog box appears.

Will sharing a printer affect my computer's performance?

When individuals on the network send files to your printer, your computer temporarily stores the files before sending them to the printer. As a result, your computer will operate more slowly while other people are using your printer.

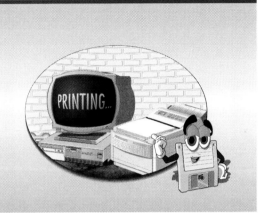

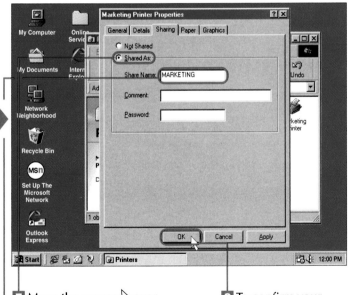

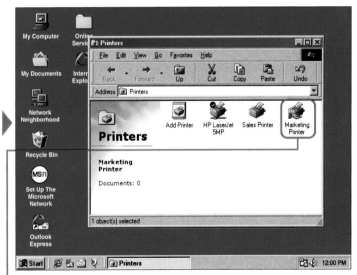

7 Move the mouse ⇧ over **Shared As:** and then press the left button (○ changes to ⊙).

■ This area displays the name of the printer people will see on the network.

8 To confirm your change, move the mouse ⇧ over **OK** and then press the left button.

■ Your printer is now available to other people on the network.

■ A hand appears under the icon for the printer you have shared.

Note: To use your printer, your colleagues must install the printer software on their computers.

■ To turn off printer sharing, repeat steps **1** to **8**, selecting **Not Shared** in step **7**.

You can easily browse through the information available on your network.

A network consists of one or more groups of computers, called workgroups. The computers in a workgroup frequently share resources, such as a printer.

BROWSE THROUGH A NETWORK

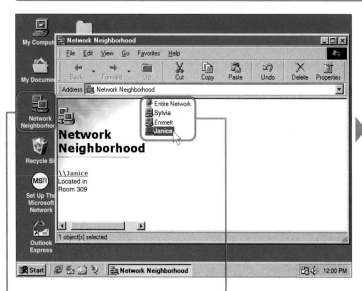

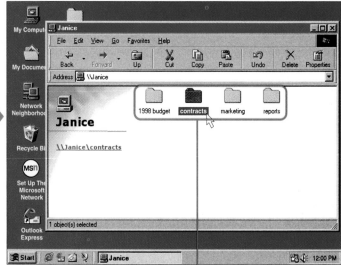

1 Move the mouse ⬚ over **Network Neighborhood** and then quickly press the left button twice.

■ The Network Neighborhood window appears, displaying all the computers in your workgroup.

2 Move the mouse ⬚ over the computer containing the files you want to work with and then quickly press the left button twice.

*Note: To view other computers on the network, select **Entire Network** in step 2.*

■ The folders shared by the computer appear.

3 Move the mouse ⬚ over the folder containing the files you want to work with and then quickly press the left button twice.

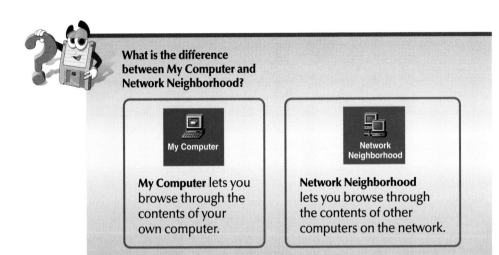

What is the difference between My Computer and Network Neighborhood?

My Computer lets you browse through the contents of your own computer.

Network Neighborhood lets you browse through the contents of other computers on the network.

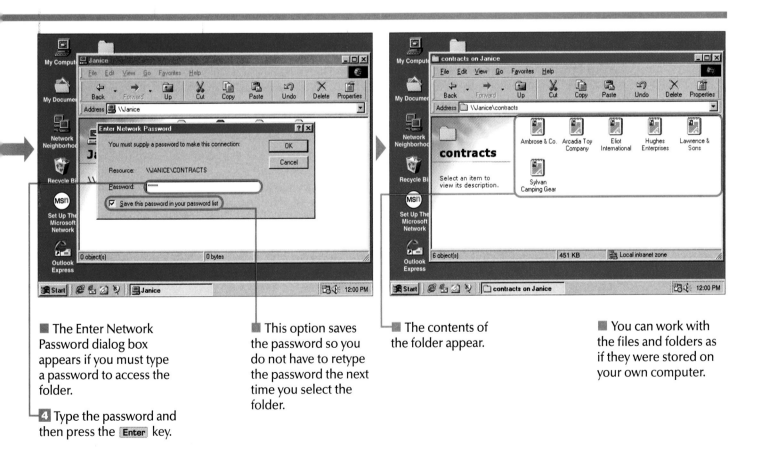

■ The Enter Network Password dialog box appears if you must type a password to access the folder.

4 Type the password and then press the Enter key.

■ This option saves the password so you do not have to retype the password the next time you select the folder.

■ The contents of the folder appear.

■ You can work with the files and folders as if they were stored on your own computer.

If you have access to more than one printer, you can choose which printer you want to automatically print your documents.

CHANGE THE DEFAULT PRINTER

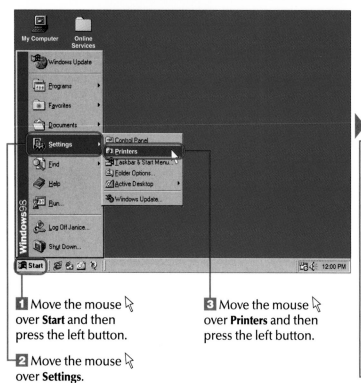

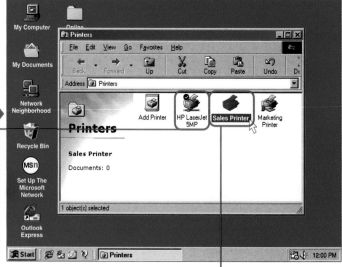

1 Move the mouse over **Start** and then press the left button.

2 Move the mouse over **Settings**.

3 Move the mouse over **Printers** and then press the left button.

■ The Printers window appears, displaying the printers you can use to print your documents.

■ The default printer displays a check mark (✔).

4 Move the mouse over the printer you want to set as your new default printer and then press the left button.

Which printer should I select as my default printer?

When selecting a default printer, you should choose the printer you use most often. The printer you select should also be close to your desk and offer the capabilities you need.

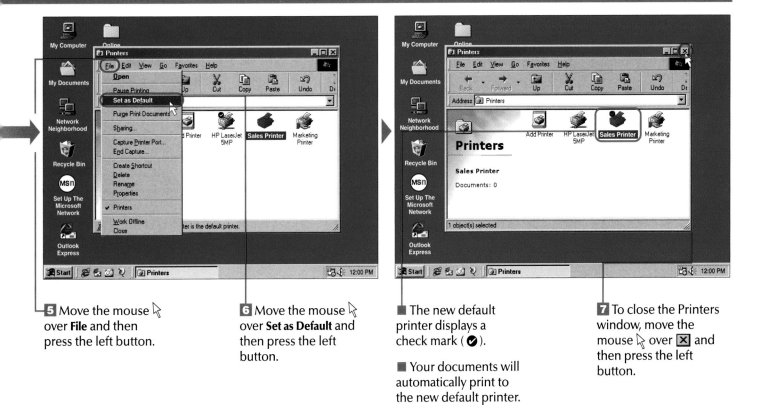

5 Move the mouse over **File** and then press the left button.

6 Move the mouse over **Set as Default** and then press the left button.

■ The new default printer displays a check mark (✓).

■ Your documents will automatically print to the new default printer.

7 To close the Printers window, move the mouse over ✕ and then press the left button.

CHAPTER 8

EXCHANGE E-MAIL

Do you want to use electronic mail? This chapter shows you how to exchange e-mail and manage your messages.

You can use Outlook Express to exchange e-mail messages with people around the world.

READ MESSAGES

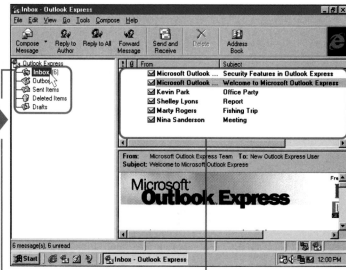

1 To start Outlook Express, move the mouse ⌖ over 📧 and then press the left button.

■ A dialog box appears if you are not connected to the Internet.

2 To connect to the Internet, move the mouse ⌖ over **Connect** and then press the left button.

Note: The Internet Connection Wizard may appear the first time you start Outlook Express to help you get connected to the Internet.

3 Move the mouse ⌖ over the folder containing the messages you want to read and then press the left button. The folder is highlighted.

■ This area displays the messages in the highlighted folder. Messages you have not read display a closed envelope (✉) and appear in bold type.

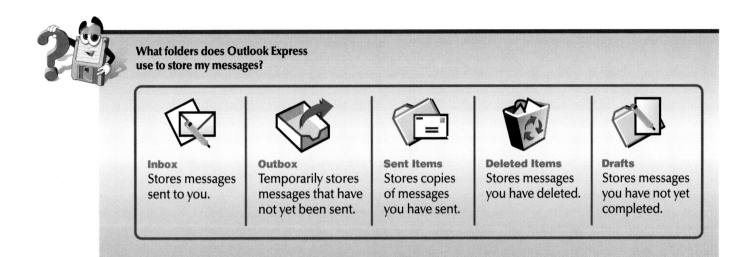

What folders does Outlook Express use to store my messages?

Inbox
Stores messages sent to you.

Outbox
Temporarily stores messages that have not yet been sent.

Sent Items
Stores copies of messages you have sent.

Deleted Items
Stores messages you have deleted.

Drafts
Stores messages you have not yet completed.

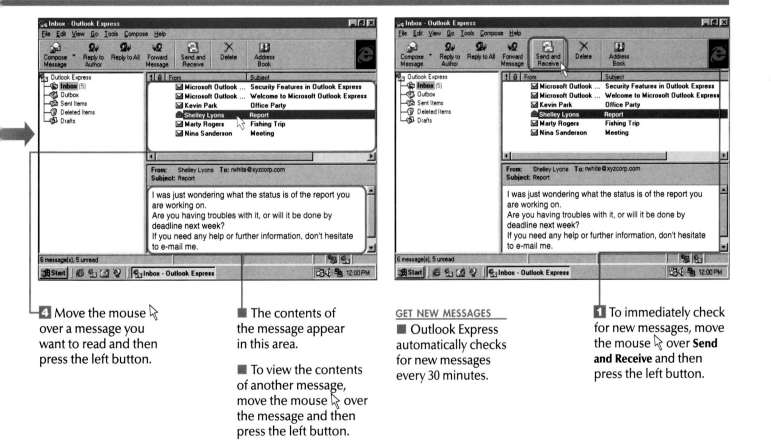

4 Move the mouse ⟋ over a message you want to read and then press the left button.

■ The contents of the message appear in this area.

■ To view the contents of another message, move the mouse ⟋ over the message and then press the left button.

GET NEW MESSAGES

■ Outlook Express automatically checks for new messages every 30 minutes.

1 To immediately check for new messages, move the mouse ⟋ over **Send and Receive** and then press the left button.

You can sort your messages to quickly find the messages you want to view.

SORT MESSAGES

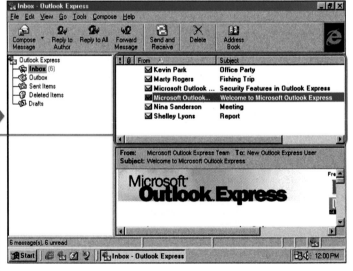

1 Move the mouse ⬚ over the heading for the column you want to use to sort the messages and then press the left button.

■ If you cannot see the heading you want to use to sort the messages, use this scroll bar to display the heading.

■ The messages appear in the new order.

■ To sort the messages in the reverse order, move the mouse ⬚ over the heading again and then press the left button.

You can produce a paper copy of a message displayed on your screen.

Outlook Express prints the page number and total number of pages at the top of each page. The current date prints at the bottom of each page.

PRINT MESSAGES

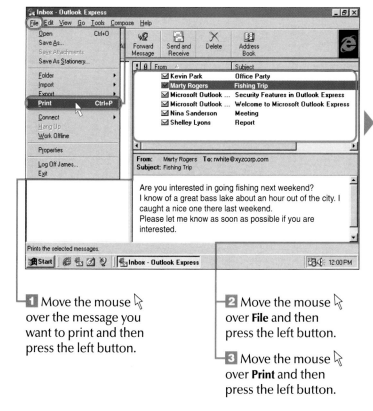

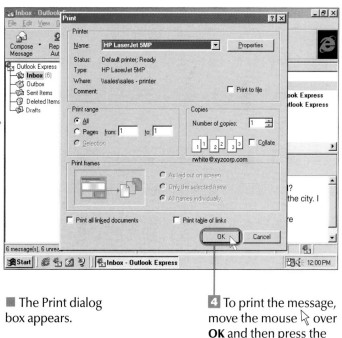

1 Move the mouse ⅄ over the message you want to print and then press the left button.

2 Move the mouse ⅄ over **File** and then press the left button.

3 Move the mouse ⅄ over **Print** and then press the left button.

■ The Print dialog box appears.

4 To print the message, move the mouse ⅄ over **OK** and then press the left button.

You can make a message appear as if you have not read the message. Marking a message as unread can help remind you to later review the message.

MARK A MESSAGE AS UNREAD

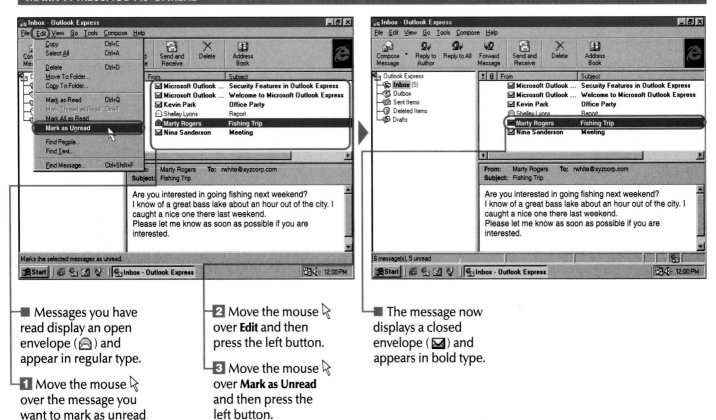

■ Messages you have read display an open envelope (📭) and appear in regular type.

1 Move the mouse ⌖ over the message you want to mark as unread and then press the left button.

2 Move the mouse ⌖ over **Edit** and then press the left button.

3 Move the mouse ⌖ over **Mark as Unread** and then press the left button.

■ The message now displays a closed envelope (✉) and appears in bold type.

CHECK FOR NEW MESSAGES AUTOMATICALLY

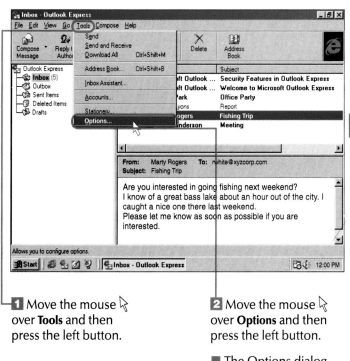

1 Move the mouse over **Tools** and then press the left button.

2 Move the mouse over **Options** and then press the left button.

■ The Options dialog box appears.

3 To check for new messages automatically, move the mouse over this option and then press the left button (☐ changes to ✔).

4 Move the mouse I over this area and then quickly press the left button twice. Then type how often you want Outlook Express to check for new messages.

5 Move the mouse I over **OK** and then press the left button.

You can compose and send a message to exchange ideas or request information.

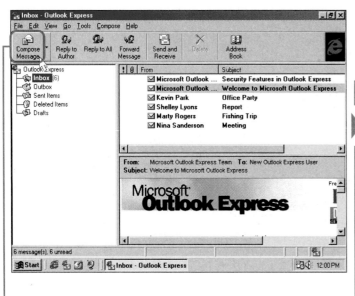

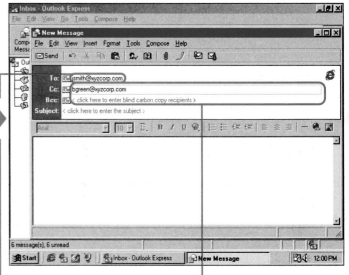

1 Move the mouse ⬐ over **Compose Message** and then press the left button.

■ The New Message window appears.

2 Type the e-mail address of the person you want to receive the message.

3 To send a copy of the message to another person, move the mouse I over one of these areas and then press the left button. Then type the e-mail address.

How can I send a message to more than one person?

Carbon Copy (Cc)
Sends an exact copy of a message to a person who would be interested in the message.

Blind Carbon Copy (Bcc)
Sends an exact copy of a message to a person without anyone else knowing that the person received the message.

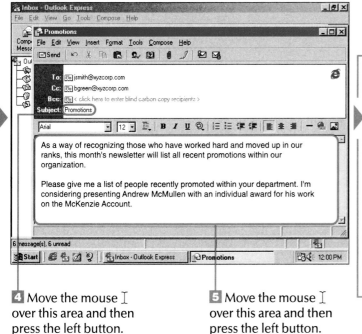

4 Move the mouse I over this area and then press the left button. Then type the subject of the message.

5 Move the mouse I over this area and then press the left button. Then type the message.

6 To send the message, move the mouse over **Send** and then press the left button.

■ Outlook Express stores a copy of each message you send in the Sent Items folder.

> You can change the design and size of text in a message to make the message more interesting and attractive.

CHANGE THE FONT

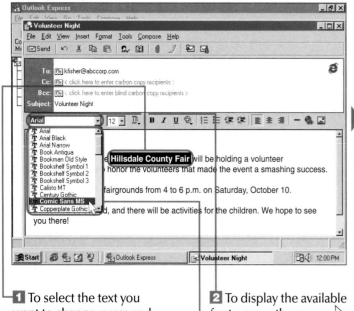

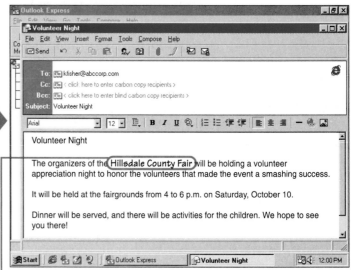

1 To select the text you want to change, press and hold down the left button as you drag the mouse I over the text until the text is highlighted.

2 To display the available fonts, move the mouse over ▼ in this area and then press the left button.

3 Move the mouse over the font you want to use and then press the left button.

■ The text changes to the new font.

■ To deselect text, move the mouse I outside the selected area and then press the left button.

Will the person receiving my message see the formatting I add to the message?

If the person you send the message to does not use Outlook Express or another e-mail program that can display formatting in messages, the message will appear without the formatting.

CHANGE THE FONT SIZE

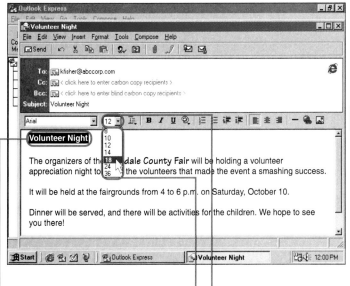

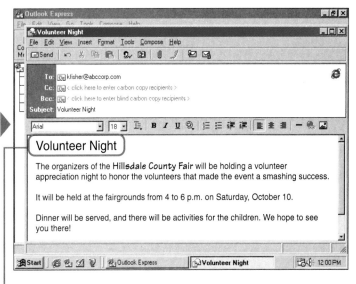

1 To select the text you want to change, press and hold down the left button as you drag the mouse I over the text until the text is highlighted.

2 To display the available font sizes, move the mouse ⬚ over ▼ in this area and then press the left button.

3 Move the mouse ⬚ over the font size you want to use and then press the left button.

■ The text changes to the new size.

■ To deselect text, move the mouse I outside the selected area and then press the left button.

You can use the bold, italic and underline styles to emphasize information in a message.

Bold
Italic
<u>Underline</u>

BOLD, ITALICIZE OR UNDERLINE TEXT

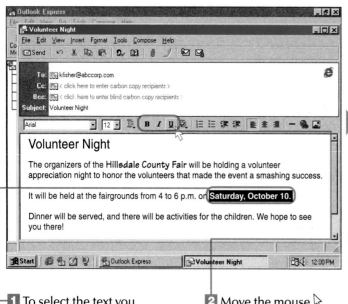

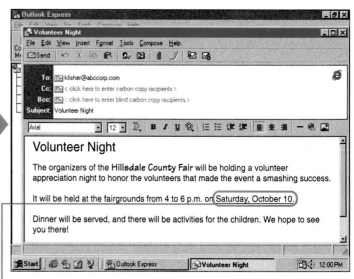

1 To select the text you want to change, press and hold down the left button as you drag the mouse I over the text until the text is highlighted.

2 Move the mouse over one of the following styles and then press the left button.

B Bold

I Italic

<u>U</u> Underline

■ The text appears in the new style.

■ To deselect text, move the mouse I outside the selected area and then press the left button.

■ To remove a bold, italic or underline style, repeat steps **1** and **2**.

You can change the color of text in a message to draw attention to important information.

ADD COLOR

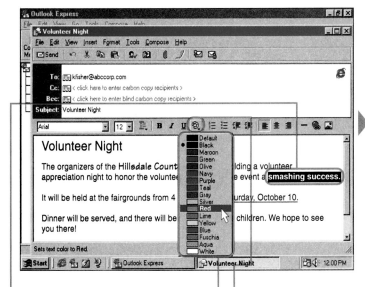

Sets text color to Red.

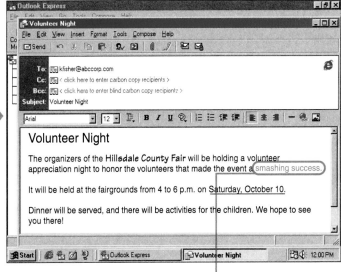

1 To select the text you want to change, press and hold down the left button as you drag the mouse I over the text until the text is highlighted.

2 To display the available colors, move the mouse ⌖ over 🖌, and then press the left button.

3 Move the mouse ⌖ over the color you want to use and then press the left button.

■ To deselect text, move the mouse I outside the selected area and then press the left button.

■ The text appears in the color you selected.

You can have Outlook Express add information about yourself to the end of every message you send. A signature saves you from having to type the same information every time you send a message.

ADD A SIGNATURE TO MESSAGES

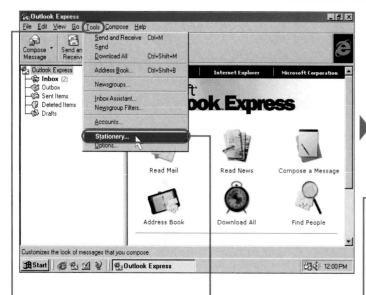

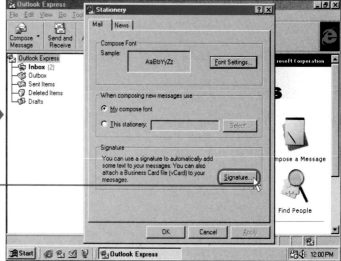

1 Move the mouse ⬡ over **Tools** and then press the left button.

2 Move the mouse ⬡ over **Stationery** and then press the left button.

■ The Stationery dialog box appears.

3 To create a signature, move the mouse ⬡ over **Signature** and then press the left button.

■ The Signature dialog box appears.

What can I include in a signature?

A signature can include information such as your name, e-mail address, occupation, favorite quotation or Web page address. You can also use plain characters to display simple pictures.

As a courtesy to people who will read your messages, do not create a signature that is more than four lines long.

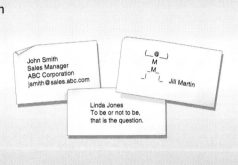

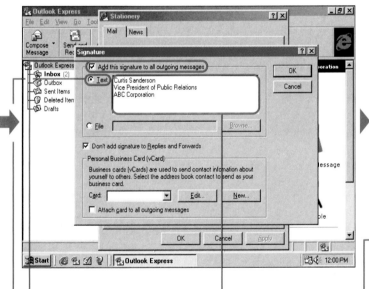

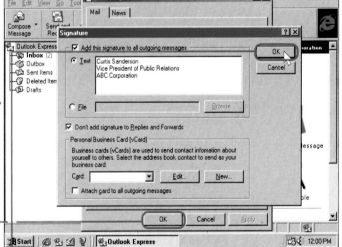

4 To add a signature to your messages, move the mouse ⇧ over this option and then press the left button (☐ changes to ☑).

5 To type your signature, move the mouse ⇧ over this option and then press the left button (◯ changes to ◉).

6 Move the mouse I over this area and then press the left button. Then type your signature.

7 To confirm your changes, move the mouse ⇧ over **OK** and then press the left button.

8 To close the Stationery dialog box, move the mouse ⇧ over **OK** and then press the left button.

■ If you no longer want to add a signature to your messages, perform steps 1 to 4 (☑ changes to ☐ in step 4). Then perform steps 7 and 8.

If you are unable to finish composing a message, you can save a draft of the message. You can then finish and send the message at a later time.

SEND LATER

SAVE A DRAFT

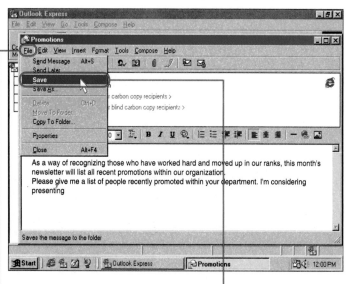

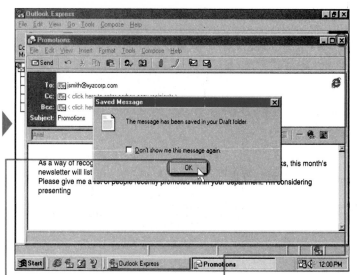

1 To compose a message, perform steps **1** to **5** starting on page 154.

2 Move the mouse over **File** and then press the left button.

3 Move the mouse over **Save** and then press the left button.

■ A dialog box appears, telling you the message was saved in your Drafts folder.

4 To close the dialog box, move the mouse over **OK** and then press the left button.

5 To close the **message**, move the mouse over ☒ and then press the left button.

Can I delete a draft message I no longer want to send?

Outlook Express stores draft messages in the Drafts folder until you complete and send the messages. If you no longer want to send a draft message, you can delete the message. To delete a message, move the mouse ⟍ over the message and then press the left button. Then press the Delete key.

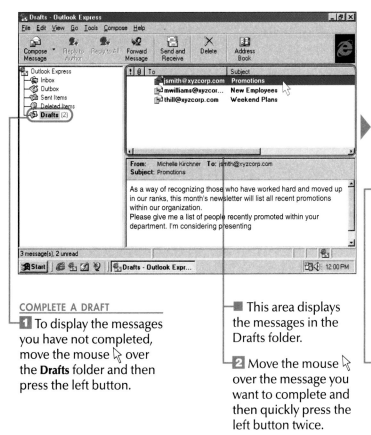

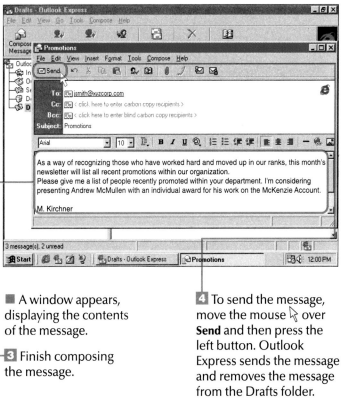

COMPLETE A DRAFT

■1 To display the messages you have not completed, move the mouse ⟍ over the **Drafts** folder and then press the left button.

■ This area displays the messages in the Drafts folder.

■2 Move the mouse ⟍ over the message you want to complete and then quickly press the left button twice.

■ A window appears, displaying the contents of the message.

■3 Finish composing the message.

■4 To send the message, move the mouse ⟍ over **Send** and then press the left button. Outlook Express sends the message and removes the message from the Drafts folder.

FIND MESSAGES

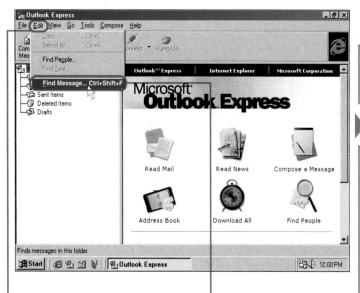

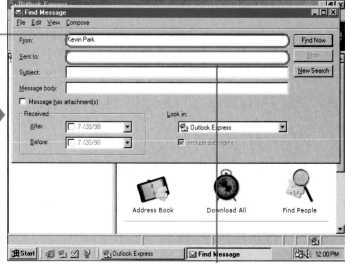

1 Move the mouse ⬚ over **Edit** and then press the left button.

2 Move the mouse ⬚ over **Find Message** and then press the left button.

■ The Find Message window appears.

3 To find messages you received from a specific person, move the mouse I over this area and then press the left button. Then type the name of the person.

4 To find messages you sent to a specific person, move the mouse I over this area and then press the left button. Then type the name of the person.

How can I search for messages?

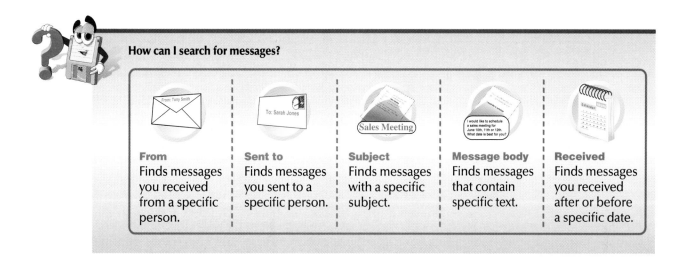

From
Finds messages you received from a specific person.

Sent to
Finds messages you sent to a specific person.

Subject
Finds messages with a specific subject.

Message body
Finds messages that contain specific text.

Received
Finds messages you received after or before a specific date.

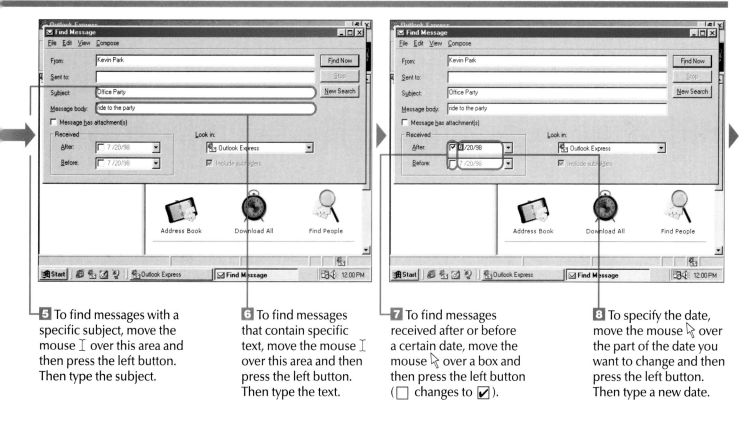

5 To find messages with a specific subject, move the mouse I over this area and then press the left button. Then type the subject.

6 To find messages that contain specific text, move the mouse I over this area and then press the left button. Then type the text.

7 To find messages received after or before a certain date, move the mouse ↕ over a box and then press the left button (☐ changes to ☑).

8 To specify the date, move the mouse ↕ over the part of the date you want to change and then press the left button. Then type a new date.

CONTINUED

When the search is complete, Outlook Express displays a list of messages that match the information you specified. You can open and review any of these messages.

FIND MESSAGES (CONTINUED)

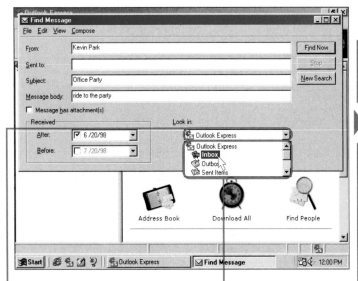

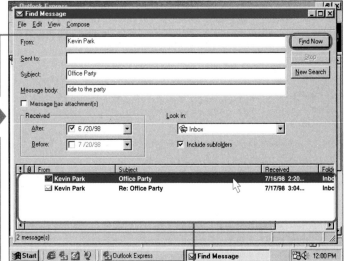

9 To select which folder you want to search, move the mouse 🔨 over this area and then press the left button.

10 Move the mouse 🔨 over the folder you want to search and then press the left button.

*Note: To search all folders, choose **Outlook Express**.*

11 To start the search, move the mouse 🔨 over **Find Now** and then press the left button.

■ This area lists the messages that match the information you specified.

12 To display the contents of a message, move the mouse 🔨 over the message and then quickly press the left button twice.

Outlook Express found a long list of messages. How can I quickly locate the message I want?

If the Find Message window displays a long list of messages, you can sort the messages by name, subject, date or folder to quickly locate the message you want to view.

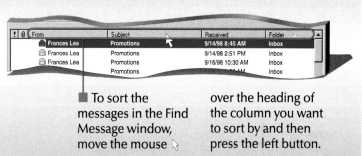

■ To sort the messages in the Find Message window, move the mouse ⌖

over the heading of the column you want to sort by and then press the left button.

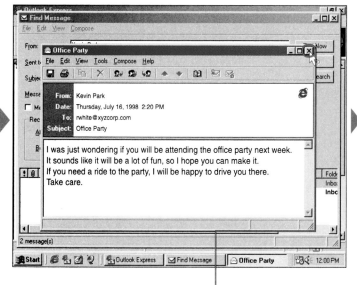

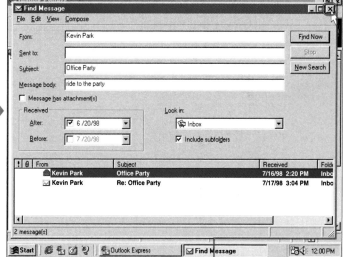

■ A window appears, displaying the contents of the message.

13 When you finish reviewing the message, move the mouse ⌖ over ✗ and then press the left button to close the message window.

■ You can repeat steps 12 and 13 to view the contents of other messages.

14 When you finish reviewing the messages, move the mouse ⌖ over ✗ and then press the left button to close the Find Message window.

NEWSGROUP MESSAGES

Does anyone know where I can find a used Postscript printer in the greater Los Angeles area?

Last night I broke my mother's prized Elvis statue. She bought it at the Graceland gift shop in 1980. Where can I get one before she notices?

I will be traveling to Las Vegas on business and was wondering if anyone can recommend a cheap hotel.

CHAPTER 9

USING NEWSGROUPS

Are you wondering how to participate in newsgroups? In this chapter you will learn how to subscribe to newsgroups, read messages and compose your own messages.

There are thousands of newsgroups on every subject imaginable. Each newsgroup discusses a particular topic, such as jobs offered, puzzles or medicine.

Newsgroup Names

The name of a newsgroup describes the type of information discussed in the newsgroup. A newsgroup name consists of two or more words, separated by dots (.).

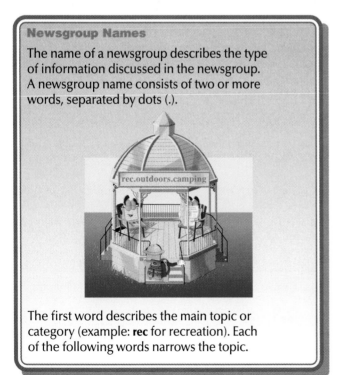

The first word describes the main topic or category (example: **rec** for recreation). Each of the following words narrows the topic.

News Servers

A news server is a computer that stores newsgroup messages. Most news servers are maintained by service providers, which are companies that give you access to the Internet.

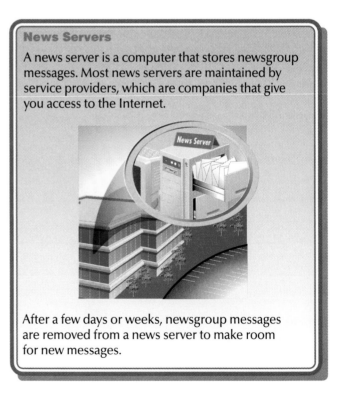

After a few days or weeks, newsgroup messages are removed from a news server to make room for new messages.

MAIN NEWSGROUP CATEGORIES

alt (alternative)

General interest discussions that can include unusual and bizarre topics. Some newsgroups include alt.fan.actors, alt.music.alternative and alt.ufo.reports.

biz (business)

Business discussions that are usually more commercial in nature than those in other newsgroups. Some newsgroups include biz.books, biz.jobs.offered and biz.marketplace.services.

comp (computers)

Discussions of computer hardware, software and computer science. Some newsgroups include comp.graphics, comp.security.misc and comp.sys.laptops.

misc (miscellaneous)

Discussions of various topics that may overlap topics discussed in other categories. Some newsgroups include misc.consumers.house, misc.education and misc.forsale.

rec (recreation)

Discussions of recreational activities and hobbies. Some newsgroups include rec.arts.movies.reviews, rec.autos and rec.food.recipes.

sci (science)

Discussions about science, including research, applied science and the social sciences. Some newsgroups include sci.agriculture, sci.energy and sci.physics.

soc (social)

Discussions of social issues, including world cultures and political topics. Some newsgroups include soc.college, soc.history and soc.women.

talk

Debates and long discussions, often about controversial subjects. Some newsgroups include talk.environment, talk.politics and talk.rumors.

You can subscribe to newsgroups you want to read on a regular basis. Outlook Express provides a list of all the available newsgroups so you can find newsgroups of interest.

SUBSCRIBE TO NEWSGROUPS

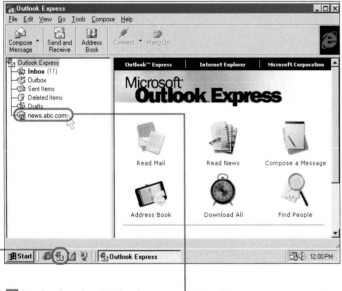

1 To display the Outlook Express window, move the mouse ▷ over 🖳 and then press the left button.

Note: If you are not connected to the Internet, a dialog box may appear that allows you to connect.

2 Move the mouse ▷ over your news server and then press the left button.

■ A dialog box appears if you are not subscribed to any newsgroups.

3 To view a list of the available newsgroups, move the mouse ▷ over **Yes** and then press the left button.

■ If the dialog box does not appear, move the mouse ▷ over **News groups** and then press the left button to view the list.

Why is my newsgroup list different from the list shown below?

The newsgroups available to you depend on the news server you use. The available newsgroups may be limited to save valuable storage space on the server.

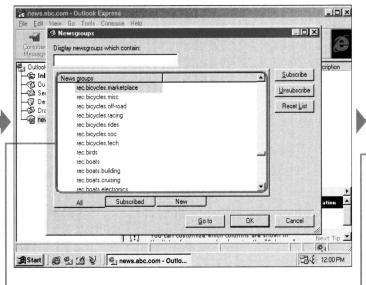

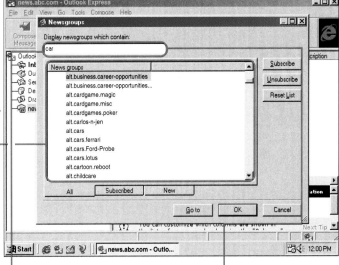

■ The Newsgroups window appears.

■ This area displays an alphabetical list of all the available newsgroups. You can use the scroll bar to browse through the list.

Note: The newsgroup list may take a few minutes to appear the first time you display the list.

4 To find newsgroup names containing a word of interest, move the mouse I over this area and then press the left button. Then type the word.

■ This area displays newsgroup names containing the word.

■ To display the entire newsgroup list, move the mouse I over this area and then quickly press the left button twice. Then press the Delete key.

CONTINUED➡

There are newsgroups on every subject imaginable. You can subscribe to newsgroups on subjects such as football, investments and stamp collecting.

SUBSCRIBE TO NEWSGROUPS (CONTINUED)

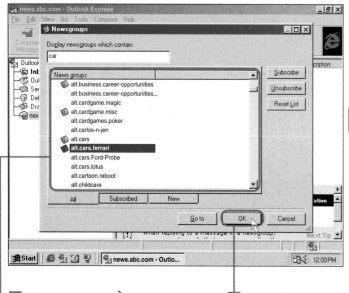

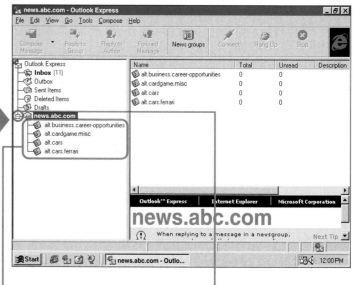

5 Move the mouse over each newsgroup you want to subscribe to and then quickly press the left button twice. A symbol (📰) appears beside each newsgroup.

6 To confirm your selections, move the mouse over **OK** and then press the left button.

■ This area displays a list of the newsgroups you are subscribed to.

■ If you cannot see a list of the newsgroups you are subscribed to, move the mouse over the plus sign (⊞) beside the news server and then press the left button (⊞ changes to ⊟).

Are there any newsgroups that can help me get started?

The following newsgroups provide useful information for beginners and let you ask questions about newsgroups:

news.answers

news.newusers.questions

UNSUBSCRIBE FROM A NEWSGROUP

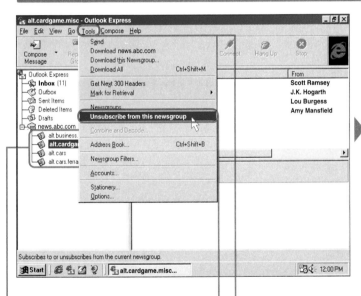

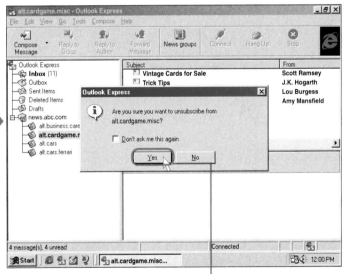

You can unsubscribe from a newsgroup if the topic no longer interests you.

◀1 Move the mouse ⬚ over the newsgroup you want to unsubscribe from and then press the left button.

2 Move the mouse ⬚ over **Tools** and then press the left button.

3 Move the mouse ⬚ over **Unsubscribe from this newsgroup** and then press the left button.

■ A warning message appears, asking if you are sure you want to unsubscribe from the newsgroup.

4 To unsubscribe from the newsgroup, move the mouse ⬚ over **Yes** and then press the left button.

■ The newsgroup disappears.

READ MESSAGES

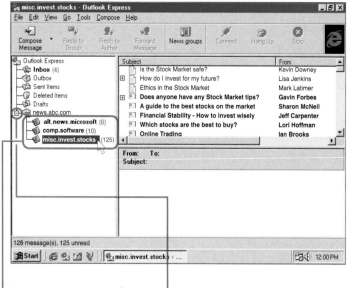

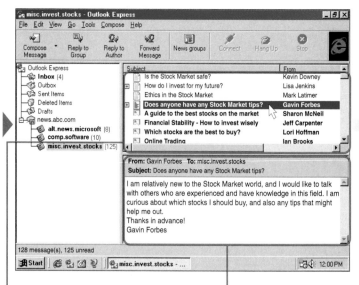

■1 Move the mouse over a newsgroup containing messages you want to read and then press the left button.

Note: The number beside the newsgroup indicates how many unread messages the newsgroup contains.

■ If you cannot see the newsgroups you are subscribed to, move the mouse over the plus sign (⊞) beside your news server and then press the left button (⊞ changes to ⊟).

■ This area displays the messages in the newsgroup. Messages you have not read appear in **bold** type.

■2 Move the mouse over a message you want to read and then press the left button.

■ The contents of the message appear in this area.

■ To view the contents of another message, move the mouse over the message and then press the left button.

Where can I find a list of questions that are commonly asked in a newsgroup?

Many newsgroups include a FAQ (Frequently Asked Questions), which is a message containing a list of questions and answers that regularly appear in a newsgroup. The FAQ is designed to prevent new readers from asking questions that have already been answered. The **news.answers** newsgroup provides FAQs for a wide variety of newsgroups.

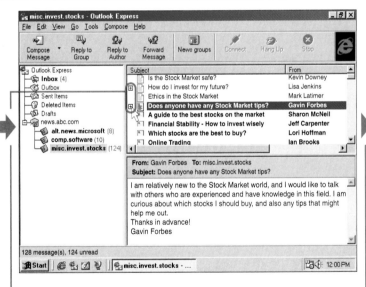

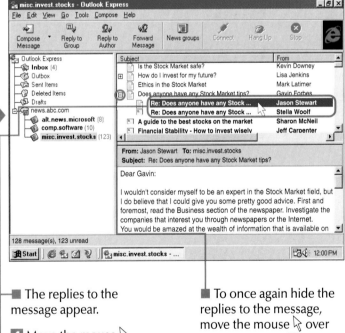

3 A plus sign (⊞) beside a message indicates that there are replies to the message. To display the replies to the message, move the mouse ⇖ over the plus sign (⊞) and then press the left button (⊞ changes to ⊟).

■ The replies to the message appear.

4 Move the mouse ⇖ over the message you want to read and then press the left button.

■ To once again hide the replies to the message, move the mouse ⇖ over the minus sign (⊟) beside the message and then press the left button (⊟ changes to ⊞).

You can reply to a newsgroup message to answer a question, express an opinion or offer additional information.

Reply to a message only when you have something important to say. A reply such as "Me too" or "I agree" is not very informative.

REPLY TO A MESSAGE

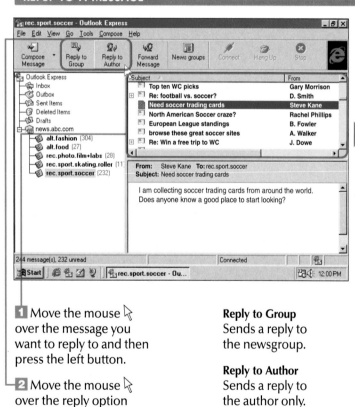

1 Move the mouse ⬏ over the message you want to reply to and then press the left button.

2 Move the mouse ⬏ over the reply option you want to use and then press the left button.

Reply to Group
Sends a reply to the newsgroup.

Reply to Author
Sends a reply to the author only.

■ A window appears for you to compose the message.

■ Outlook Express fills in the newsgroup name or e-mail address for you.

■ Outlook Express also fills in the subject, starting the subject with **Re:**

Who can I send a reply to?

You can send a reply to the newsgroup or just the author of the message. Send a message to just the author when your reply would not be of interest to others in the newsgroup or if you want to send a private response.

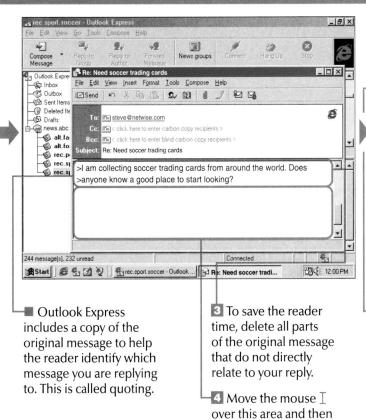

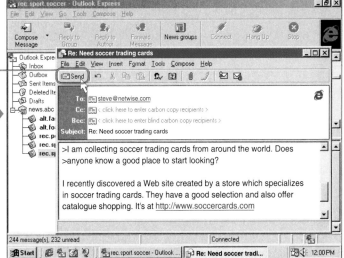

■ Outlook Express includes a copy of the original message to help the reader identify which message you are replying to. This is called quoting.

3 To save the reader time, delete all parts of the original message that do not directly relate to your reply.

4 Move the mouse I over this area and then press the left button. Then type your reply.

5 To send your reply, move the mouse ⬦ over **Send** or **Post** and then press the left button.

Note: The appearance of this button depends on the reply option you selected in step 2.

■ A dialog box may appear, stating that your reply was sent to the news server. Move the mouse ⬦ over **OK** and then press the left button.

You can compose and send a new message to a newsgroup to ask a question or express an opinion.

I heard that Bob Tielemans was recently inducted into the Rock & Roll Hall of Fame in Cleveland, Ohio. Could someone tell me what other guitar players have been inducted?

Thanks,
Sean Brady

When sending a new message to a newsgroup, keep in mind that thousands of people around the world may read the message.

If you want to practice sending a message, send one to the **misc.test** newsgroup. Do not send practice messages to other newsgroups.

COMPOSE A MESSAGE

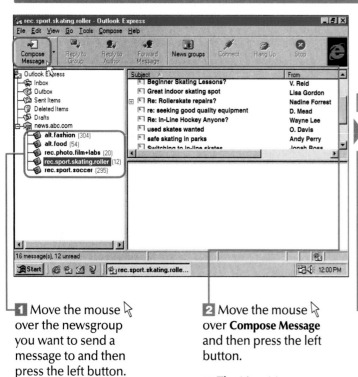

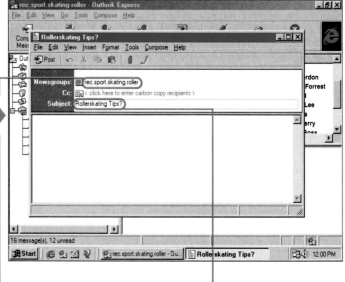

1 Move the mouse over the newsgroup you want to send a message to and then press the left button.

2 Move the mouse over **Compose Message** and then press the left button.

■ The New Message window appears.

■ Outlook Express fills in the name of the newsgroup for you.

3 Type a subject for the message. Make sure the subject clearly identifies the contents of your message.

Should I read the messages in a newsgroup before sending a new message?

Reading the messages in a newsgroup without participating is known as lurking. Lurking helps you avoid sending information others have already read and is a great way to learn how people in a newsgroup communicate. You should lurk in a newsgroup for at least one week before sending a new message.

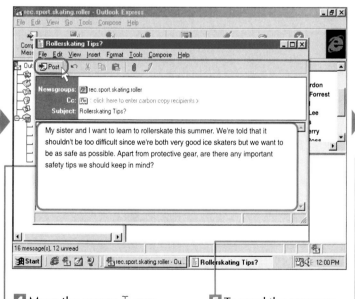

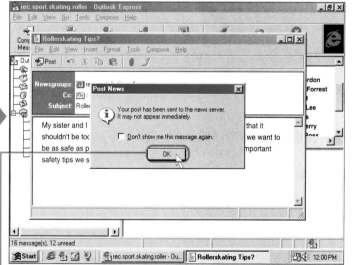

■4 Move the mouse I over this area and then press the left button. Then type the message. Make sure the message is clear, concise and does not contain spelling or grammar errors.

■5 To send the message, move the mouse ⟲ over **Post** and then press the left button.

■ A dialog box appears, stating that your message has been sent to the news server.

■6 To close the dialog box, move the mouse ⟲ over **OK** and then press the left button.

■ Outlook Express stores a copy of each message you send in the Sent Items folder.

CHAPTER 10

USING NETMEETING

Do you want to communicate and work with other people over the Internet? After reading this chapter you will be able to exchange information and share programs using NetMeeting.

> NetMeeting allows you to communicate with other people on the Internet.

You can use NetMeeting to exchange messages and work on documents with other people.

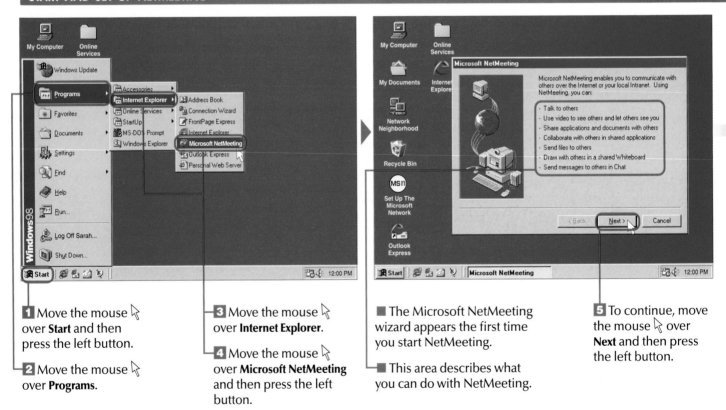

1 Move the mouse ⬀ over **Start** and then press the left button.

2 Move the mouse ⬀ over **Programs**.

3 Move the mouse ⬀ over **Internet Explorer**.

4 Move the mouse ⬀ over **Microsoft NetMeeting** and then press the left button.

■ The Microsoft NetMeeting wizard appears the first time you start NetMeeting.

■ This area describes what you can do with NetMeeting.

5 To continue, move the mouse ⬀ over **Next** and then press the left button.

How can other NetMeeting users contact me?

Windows can include your name in a directory that everyone using NetMeeting can view. The directory shows your e-mail address, first name, last name, city/state, country and comments. The information that appears in the directory depends on the information you enter in the Microsoft NetMeeting wizard.

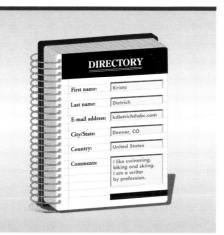

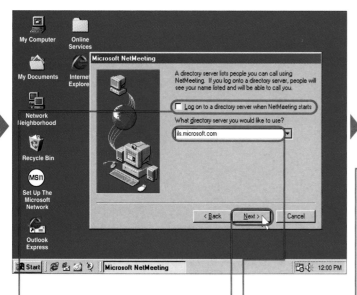

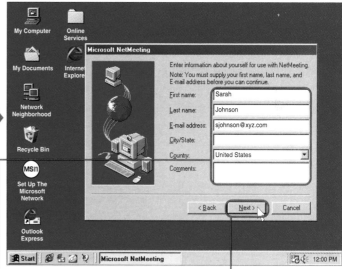

■6 If you do not want your name to appear in a directory of NetMeeting users, move the mouse ₧ over this option and then press the left button (☑ changes to ☐).

■ This area displays the directory server you will use.

■7 To continue, move the mouse ₧ over **Next** and then press the left button.

■8 To enter your information, move the mouse I over each area and then press the left button. Then type the appropriate information.

Note: You only need to supply your first name, last name and e-mail address to continue.

■9 To continue, move the mouse ₧ over **Next** and then press the left button.

CONTINUED➡

You can choose to categorize your information as personal, business or adults-only.

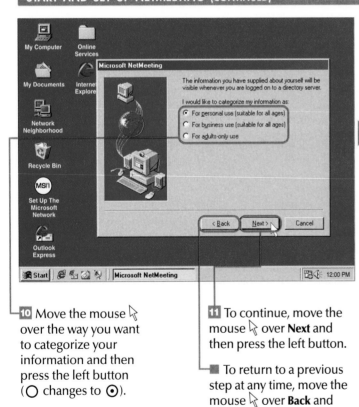

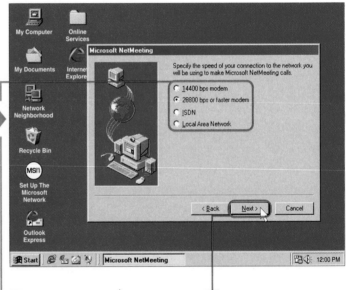

10 Move the mouse � over the way you want to categorize your information and then press the left button (○ changes to ⊙).

11 To continue, move the mouse ⍳ over **Next** and then press the left button.

■ To return to a previous step at any time, move the mouse ⍳ over **Back** and then press the left button.

12 Move the mouse ⍳ over the type of connection you will use to make NetMeeting calls and then press the left button (○ changes to ⊙).

13 To continue, move the mouse ⍳ over **Next** and then press the left button.

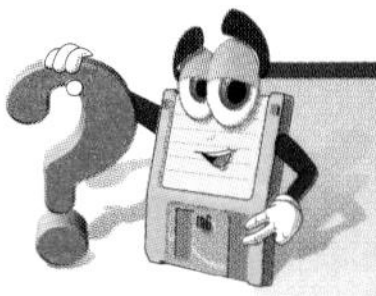

What equipment do I need to hear sound when using NetMeeting?

You need a sound card and speakers to hear sound when using NetMeeting. You need a microphone to talk to another person. Only two people in a meeting can use microphones to communicate.

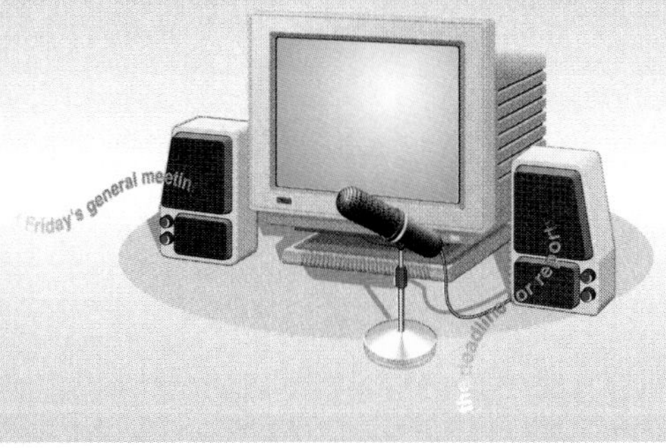

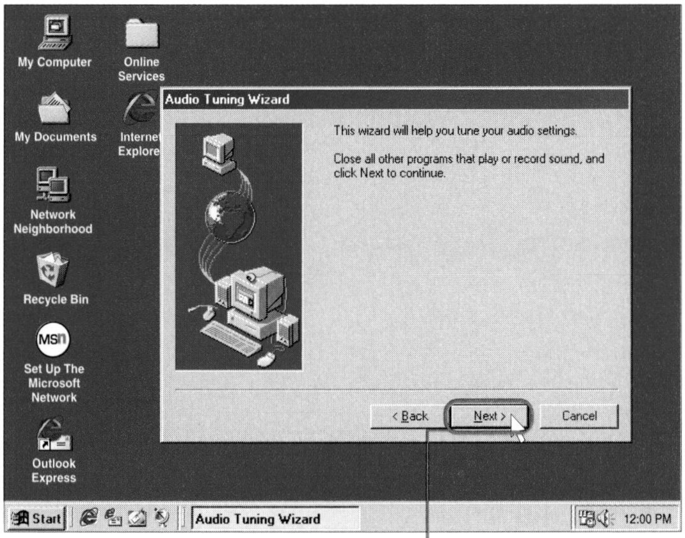

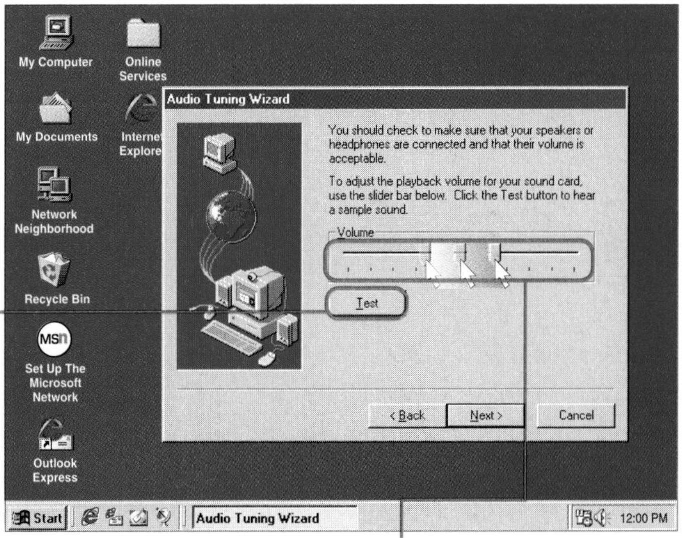

- The wizard will now help you adjust your audio settings.

- Make sure you close all programs that play or record sound before continuing.

14 To continue, move the mouse over **Next** and then press the left button.

15 To hear a sample sound, move the mouse over **Test** and then press the left button.

16 To adjust the volume, position the mouse over the slider ( ) and then press and hold down the left button as you drag the slider left or right.

CONTINUED

START AND SET UP NETMEETING

The wizard will make sure your microphone is working and the volume is at an acceptable level.

START AND SET UP NETMEETING (CONTINUED)

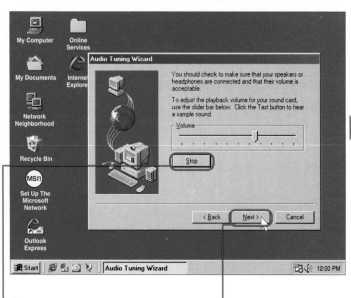

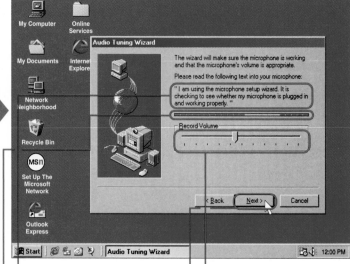

17 When you finish adjusting the volume, move the mouse ⇗ over **Stop** and then press the left button to stop playing the sample sound.

18 To continue, move the mouse ⇗ over **Next** and then press the left button.

19 Read this text into your microphone.

■ This area indicates the microphone's volume. The color should extend into the normal (yellow) range.

20 To adjust the volume, position the mouse ⇗ over the slider (▯) and then press and hold down the left button as you drag the slider left or right.

21 Move the mouse ⇗ over **Next** and then press the left button.

Can I use NetMeeting to send video images?

You can use NetMeeting to send a video image of yourself to the person you contact. You need a video capture card and camera or a camera that supports Video for Windows. If you do not have any video equipment, you can still receive video images from other people.

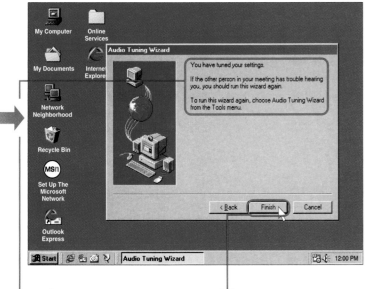

■ This message appears when the setup is complete.

22 To start NetMeeting, move the mouse ⬚ over **Finish** and then press the left button.

■ The Microsoft NetMeeting window appears.

You can place a call to contact another person on the Internet.

The person you want to call must have NetMeeting open on their computer.

PLACE A CALL

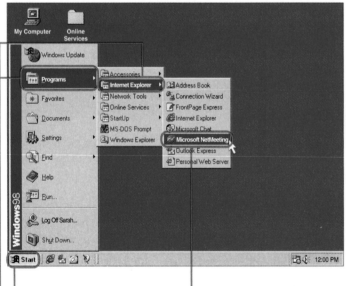

1 Move the mouse ᐅ over **Start** and then press the left button.

2 Move the mouse ᐅ over **Programs**.

3 Move the mouse ᐅ over **Internet Explorer**.

4 Move the mouse ᐅ over **Microsoft NetMeeting** and then press the left button.

■ The Microsoft NetMeeting window appears.

Note: If you are not connected to the Internet, a dialog box will appear that allows you to connect.

5 To view a list of people you can contact, move the mouse ᐅ over **Directory** and then press the left button.

■ This area displays information about each person you can contact.

■ To sort the names, move the mouse ᐅ over the heading for the column you want to sort by and then press the left button.

What do the symbols beside the names in the directory mean?

Person is in a call.

Person is not in a call.

Person has a microphone and speakers.

Person has a video camera.

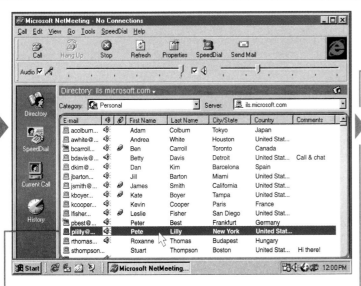

6 Move the mouse over the person you want to contact and then quickly press the left button twice.

Note: NetMeeting will ask the other person if they will accept the call.

7 Once the person accepts your call, this area lists each person in the meeting.

■ To adjust the microphone or speaker volume, position the mouse over the appropriate slider (🔲) and then press and hold down the left button as you drag the slider.

8 To end the call, move the mouse over **Hang Up** and then press the left button.

You can exchange messages with other people using NetMeeting. This is known as chatting. A message you send will instantly appear on the computer of each person in the meeting.

1 Call the person you want to chat with. See page 190 to place a call.

2 To chat with the person, move the mouse ⌖ over **Chat** and then press the left button.

■ The Chat window appears.

3 Move the mouse ⌖ over this area and then press the left button. Then type the message you want to send.

4 To send the message, move the mouse ⌖ over 🖻 and then press the left button.

Note: The other person will not see the text you type until you send the message.

Is there a faster way to communicate when using NetMeeting?

If you and the other person in the meeting both have a microphone, sound card and speakers, you can talk to each other without paying any long distance charges.

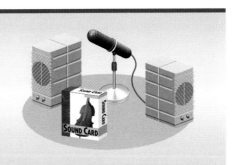

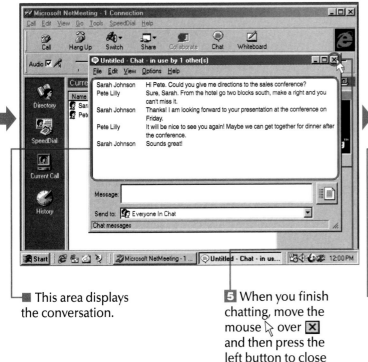

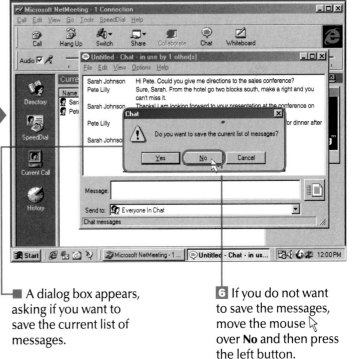

■ This area displays the conversation.

5 When you finish chatting, move the mouse ▷ over ☒ and then press the left button to close the Chat window.

■ A dialog box appears, asking if you want to save the current list of messages.

6 If you do not want to save the messages, move the mouse ▷ over **No** and then press the left button.

You can use NetMeeting to work on a Whiteboard with other people. You can draw images that will instantly appear on the computer screens of the other people in the meeting.

USING THE WHITEBOARD

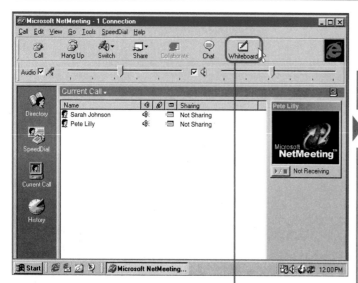

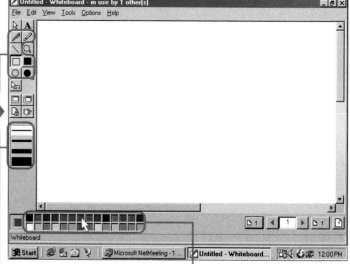

1 Call the person you want to use the Whiteboard with. See page 190 to place a call.

2 Move the mouse � over **Whiteboard** and then press the left button.

■ The Whiteboard window appears.

3 Move the mouse � over the tool for the object you want to draw and then press the left button.

4 Move the mouse � over a width for the object and then press the left button.

Note: The width options are only available for some objects.

5 Move the mouse � over a color for the object and then press the left button.

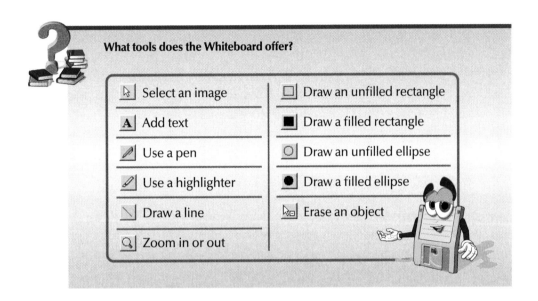

What tools does the Whiteboard offer?

⬚	Select an image	⬚	Draw an unfilled rectangle
A	Add text	■	Draw a filled rectangle
✎	Use a pen	○	Draw an unfilled ellipse
✎	Use a highlighter	●	Draw a filled ellipse
╲	Draw a line		Erase an object
⌕	Zoom in or out		

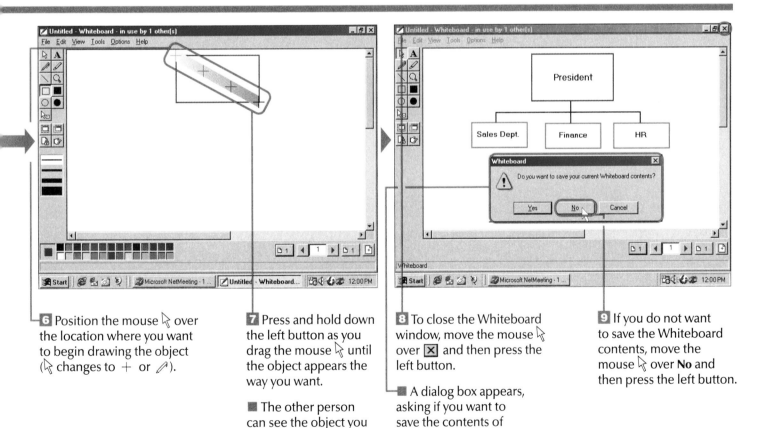

6 Position the mouse ⬚ over the location where you want to begin drawing the object (⬚ changes to + or ✎).

7 Press and hold down the left button as you drag the mouse ⬚ until the object appears the way you want.

■ The other person can see the object you created.

8 To close the Whiteboard window, move the mouse ⬚ over ✕ and then press the left button.

■ A dialog box appears, asking if you want to save the contents of the Whiteboard.

9 If you do not want to save the Whiteboard contents, move the mouse ⬚ over **No** and then press the left button.

You can use NetMeeting to work on a document with another person at the same time.

When you share a program, the other person does not need the program installed on their computer.

SHARE A PROGRAM

1 Call the person you want to share a program with. See page 190 to place a call.

2 Start the program you want to share. See page 8 to start a program.

3 Move the mouse over **Share** and then press the left button.

4 Move the mouse over the program you want to share and then press the left button.

■ A dialog box appears, stating that you have chosen to share a program.

5 To continue, move the mouse over **OK** and then press the left button.

Why would I share a program with other people?

You can share a program to teach another person how to use the program. Sharing a program is also useful when two or more people are working on the same project. Each person can view and make changes to a document at the same time. This is known as collaborating.

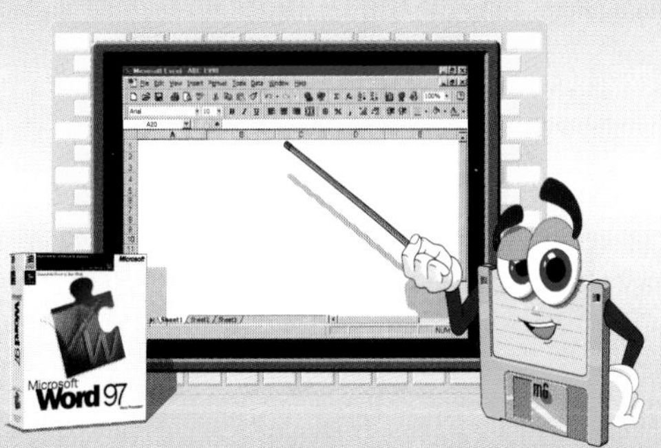

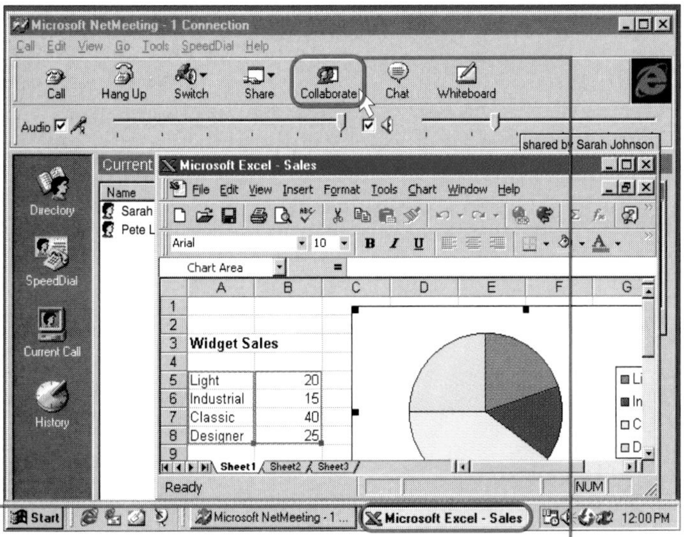

6 Move the mouse over the button on the taskbar for the program you are sharing and then press the left button.

■ The other person can see the changes you make, but cannot make changes.

7 If you want the other person to be able to make changes, move the mouse over **Collaborate** and then press the left button.

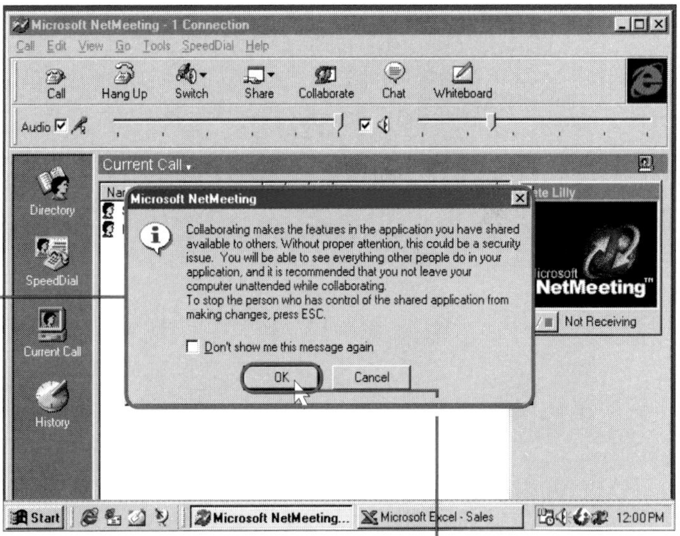

■ A dialog box appears, confirming that you are about to allow the other person to make changes to the document.

8 To continue, move the mouse over **OK** and then press the left button.

■ To stop sharing the document, repeat steps 3 and 4.

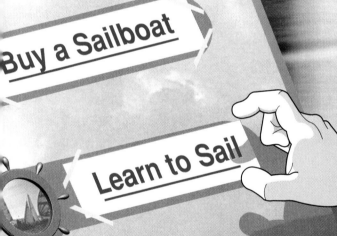

CHAPTER 11

CREATE WEB PAGES

Would you like to design your own Web page? This chapter shows you how to create and publish Web pages.

FrontPage Express allows you to create and edit Web pages. You can place Web pages you create on the Internet so people around the world can view the pages.

You can also place Web pages you create on your corporate intranet. An intranet is a small version of the Internet within a company or organization.

REASONS FOR PUBLISHING WEB PAGES

Personal

Many people use the Web to share information about a topic that interests them. You can create Web pages to discuss your favorite celebrity or hobby, show your favorite pictures, promote a club you belong to or present a résumé to potential employers.

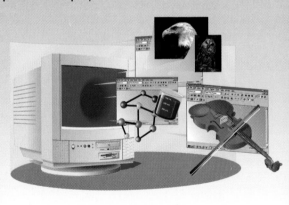

Commercial

Companies use Web pages to keep the public informed about new products, interesting news and job openings within the company. Many companies also allow readers to use the Web pages to place orders for products and services.

You can start FrontPage Express to create your own Web pages.

START FRONTPAGE EXPRESS

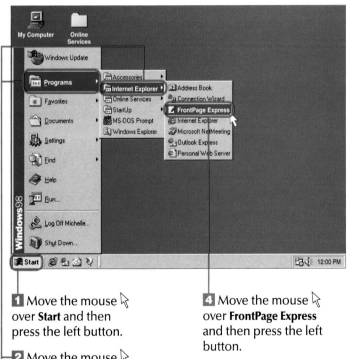

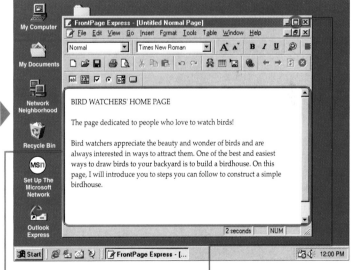

1 Move the mouse over **Start** and then press the left button.

2 Move the mouse over **Programs**.

3 Move the mouse over **Internet Explorer**.

4 Move the mouse over **FrontPage Express** and then press the left button.

■ The FrontPage Express window appears.

5 Type the text you want to appear on your Web page.

■ Press the Enter key only when you want to start a new line or paragraph.

■ To enlarge the FrontPage Express window to fill your screen, move the mouse over ▣ and then press the left button.

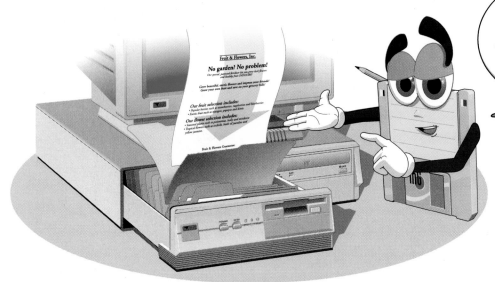

You should save a Web page you create to store the page for future use. This lets you later review and update the Web page.

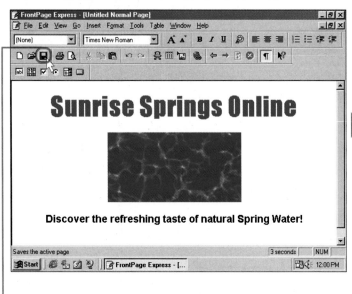

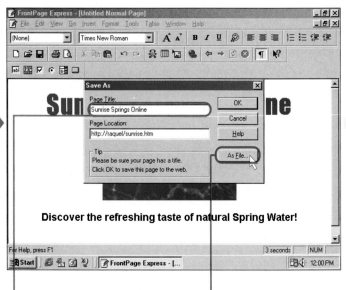

1 Move the mouse ⌖ over 🖫 and then press the left button.

■ The Save As dialog box appears.

Note: If you previously saved the Web page, the Save As dialog box will not appear.

2 Type a title for the Web page that describes the information on the page.

3 To store the Web page on your computer, move the mouse ⌖ over **As File** and then press the left button.

■ The Save As File dialog box appears.

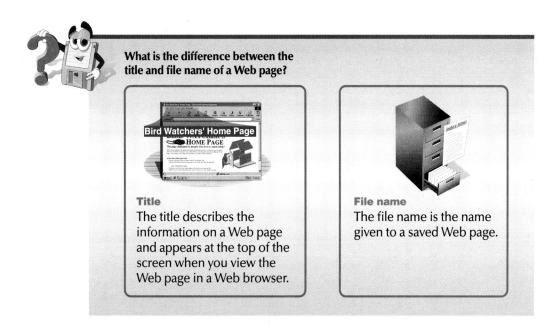

What is the difference between the title and file name of a Web page?

Title
The title describes the information on a Web page and appears at the top of the screen when you view the Web page in a Web browser.

File name
The file name is the name given to a saved Web page.

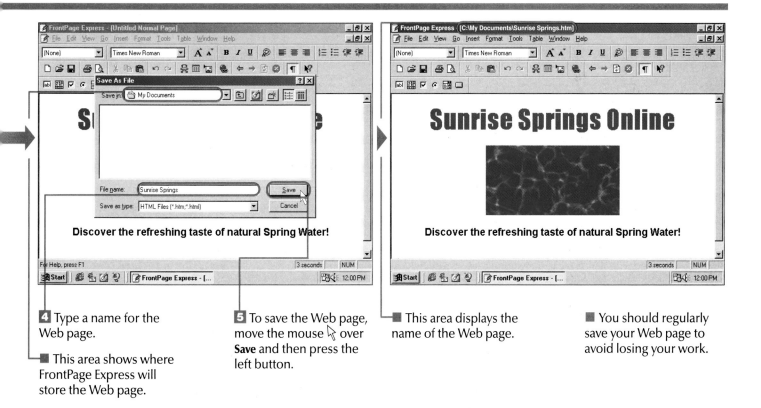

■ 4 Type a name for the Web page.

■ This area shows where FrontPage Express will store the Web page.

■ 5 To save the Web page, move the mouse ⌖ over **Save** and then press the left button.

■ This area displays the name of the Web page.

■ You should regularly save your Web page to avoid losing your work.

FORMAT TEXT

You can make your Web page look more attractive by changing the design of the text.

You can increase or decrease the size of text on your Web page.

CHANGE THE FONT

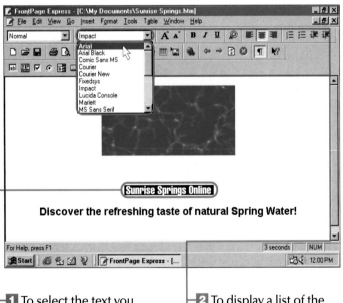

1 To select the text you want to change, press and hold down the left button as you drag the mouse I over the text until the text is highlighted.

2 To display a list of the available fonts, move the mouse ⓚ over this area and then press the left button.

3 Move the mouse ⓚ over the font you want to use and then press the left button.

CHANGE THE TEXT SIZE

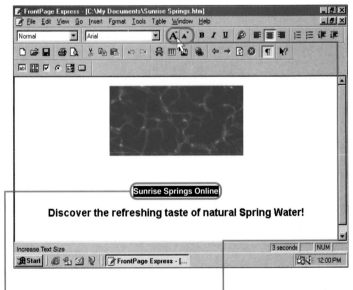

1 To select the text you want to change, press and hold down the left button as you drag the mouse I over the text until the text is highlighted.

2 Move the mouse ⓚ over the size option you want to use and then press the left button.

A⁺ Increase the text size

A⁻ Decrease the text size

You can bold, italicize or underline text to emphasize information on your Web page.

You can change the color of text on your Web page.

BOLD, ITALICIZE OR UNDERLINE TEXT

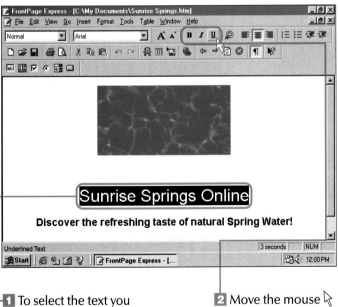

1 To select the text you want to change, press and hold down the left button as you drag the mouse I over the text until the text is highlighted.

2 Move the mouse $\&$ over the style you want to use and then press the left button.

B Bold

I Italic

U Underline

COLOR TEXT

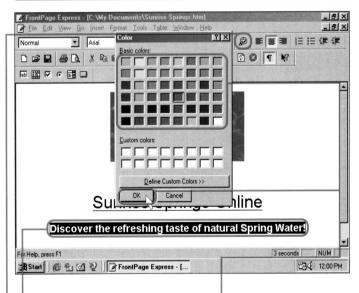

1 To select the text you want to change, press and hold down the left button as you drag the mouse I over the text until the text is highlighted.

2 Move the mouse $\&$ over 🖉 and then press the left button.

3 Move the mouse $\&$ over the color you want to use and then press the left button.

4 Move the mouse $\&$ over **OK** and then press the left button.

You can enhance the appearance of your Web page by aligning text in different ways.

You can use the Indent feature to set off paragraphs on your Web page.

My three favorite wines are:
- Chardonnay
- Riesling
- Chenin Blanc

For a free catalog, please write to:

Miller Textiles
2455 King St.
Boston, MA
02101

CHANGE TEXT ALIGNMENT

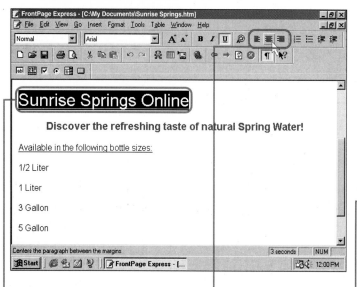

INDENT TEXT

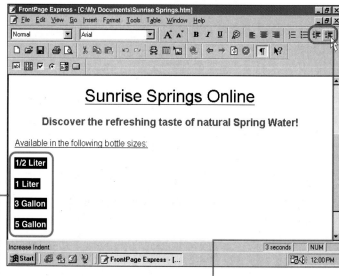

1 To select the text you want to change, press and hold down the left button as you drag the mouse I over the text until the text is highlighted.

2 Move the mouse ⬚ over the alignment option you want to use and then press the left button.

▤ Left

▤ Center

▤ Right

1 To select the text you want to indent, press and hold down the left button as you drag the mouse I over the text until the text is highlighted.

2 Move the mouse ⬚ over the indent option you want to use and then press the left button.

▤ Move text to the left

▤ Move text to the right

You can separate items in a list by beginning each item with a number or bullet.

Recipe:
1. Preheat oven to 300°F
2. Grate 1 cup of cheese
3. Dice 1/4 cup of onions
4. Slice 1/2 a red pepper into strips
5. Add cheese, onions and red pepper to meat sauce
6. Bake for 20 minutes

Shopping List:
- cheese
- onions
- red peppers
- meat
- tomato sauce

Numbers are useful for items in a specific order, such as a set of instructions. Bullets are useful for items in no particular order, such as a checklist.

CREATE A LIST

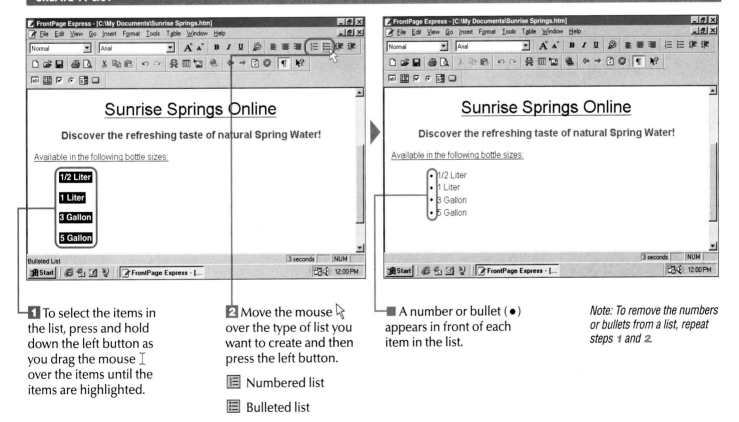

1 To select the items in the list, press and hold down the left button as you drag the mouse ⌶ over the items until the items are highlighted.

2 Move the mouse ⌖ over the type of list you want to create and then press the left button.

▤ Numbered list

▤ Bulleted list

■ A number or bullet (●) appears in front of each item in the list.

Note: To remove the numbers or bullets from a list, repeat steps 1 and 2.

> You can add images to your Web page to make the page more interesting and attractive.

When adding images to your Web page, try to use images with the .gif or .jpg extension, since these are the most common types of images on the Web.

Before adding images to your Web page, place the images you want to use in the folder where your Web page is stored.

INSERT AN IMAGE

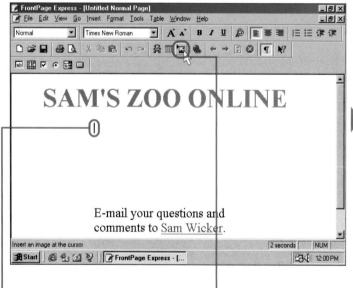

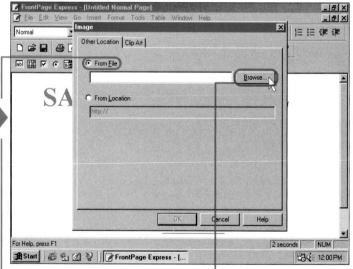

1 Move the mouse I over the location where you want the image to appear and then press the left button.

Note: The image will appear where the insertion point flashes on your screen.

2 To insert an image, move the mouse ⇖ over 🖾 and then press the left button.

■ The Image dialog box appears.

3 To select an image stored on your computer, move the mouse ⇖ over **From File** and then press the left button (○ changes to ⊙).

4 To search for the image on your computer, move the mouse ⇖ over **Browse** and then press the left button.

■ The Image dialog box appears.

Where can I get images to use in my Web pages?

Many pages on the Web offer images you can use for free or you can buy a collection of ready-made images, called clip art, at most computer stores. You can also use a scanner to scan images into your computer or use a drawing program to create your own images. Make sure you have permission to use any images you do not create yourself.

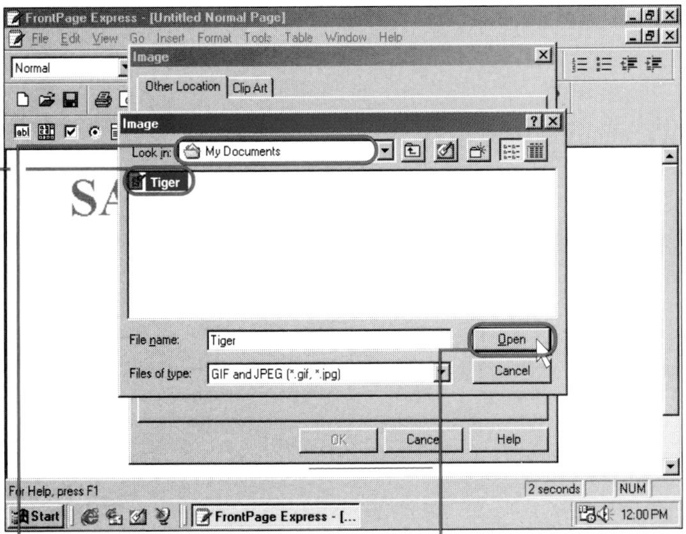

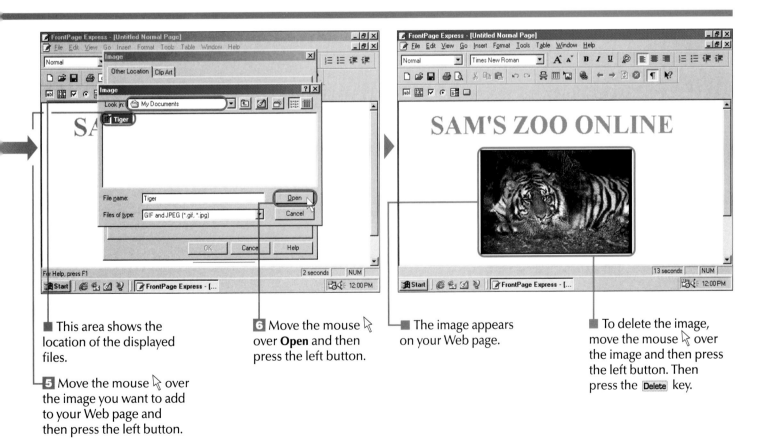

■ This area shows the location of the displayed files.

5 Move the mouse over the image you want to add to your Web page and then press the left button.

6 Move the mouse over **Open** and then press the left button.

■ The image appears on your Web page.

■ To delete the image, move the mouse over the image and then press the left button. Then press the Delete key.

ADD A BACKGROUND IMAGE

You can have a small image repeat to fill an entire Web page. This can add an interesting background texture to your page.

You can get background images at the following Web sites:

www.ecnet.net/users/gas52r0/Jay/backgrounds/back.htm

www.ender-design.com/rg/backidx.html

ADD A BACKGROUND IMAGE

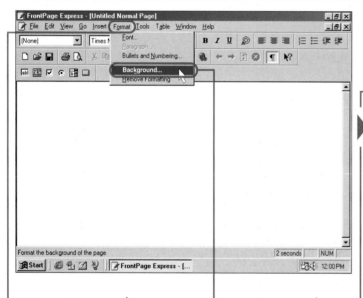

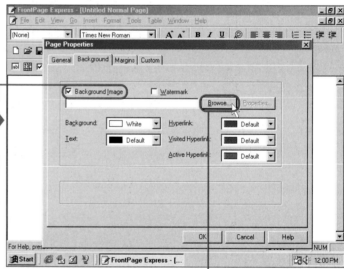

1 Move the mouse ⬚ over **Format** and then press the left button.

2 Move the mouse ⬚ over **Background** and then press the left button.

■ The Page Properties dialog box appears.

3 To use a background image, move the mouse ⬚ over this option and then press the left button (☐ changes to ☑).

4 To search for the background image you want to use, move the mouse ⬚ over **Browse** and then press the left button.

■ The Select Background Image dialog box appears.

What type of background image should I choose?

Choose an image that creates an interesting background design without overwhelming your Web page. Also make sure the image will not affect the readability of your Web page. To make the page easier to read, you may need to change the text color. See page 205 to change the color of text on a Web page.

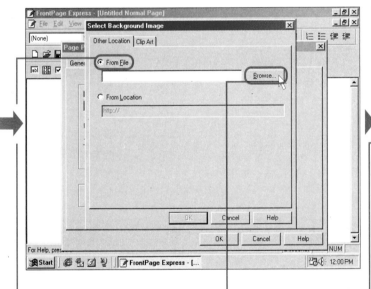

5 To select a background image stored on your computer, move the mouse ⌖ over **From File** and then press the left button (○ changes to ⊙).

6 To search for the image on your computer, move the mouse ⌖ over **Browse** and then press the left button.

■ The Select Background Image dialog box appears.

■ This area shows the location of the displayed files.

7 Move the mouse ⌖ over the background image you want to use and then press the left button.

8 Move the mouse ⌖ over **Open** and then press the left button.

9 In the Page Properties dialog box, move the mouse ⌖ over **OK** and then press the left button.

■ The background image appears.

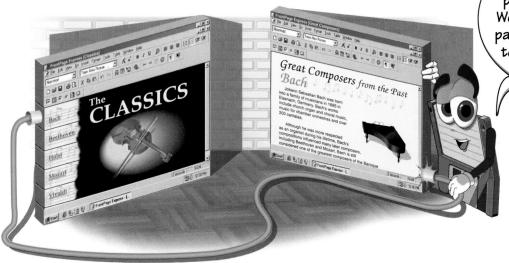

You can create a link to connect a word, phrase or image in your Web page to another Web page. When you select the text or image, the other Web page appears.

Adding links to your Web page gives readers quick access to Web pages that relate to your page.

CREATE A LINK

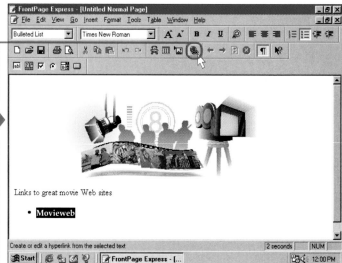

1 To select the text you want to link to another Web page, press and hold down the left button as you drag the mouse I over the text until the text is highlighted.

■ To select the image you want to link to another Web page, move the mouse ⬐ over the image and then press the left button.

2 To create a link, move the mouse ⬐ over 🔗 and then press the left button.

■ The Create Hyperlink dialog box appears.

How can I quickly create a link in my Web page?

When you type a Web page address or e-mail address, FrontPage Express automatically converts the address to a link for you.

Note: The address becomes a link after you press the `Enter` *key or* `Spacebar` .

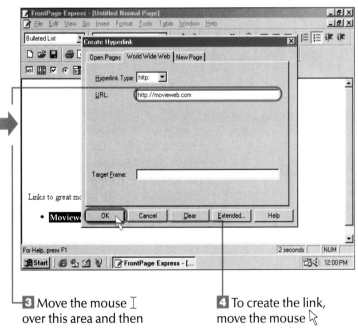

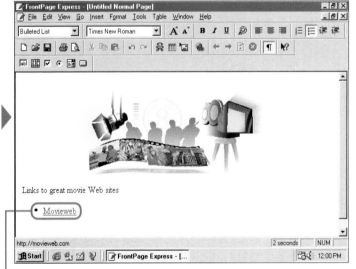

3 Move the mouse I over this area and then press the left button. Then type the address of the Web page you want to link the text or image to.

4 To create the link, move the mouse over **OK** and then press the left button.

■ FrontPage Express creates the link. Text links appear underlined and in color.

■ To deselect text, move the mouse I outside the selected area and then press the left button.

■ When you select the text or image in a Web browser, the Web page connected to the link will appear.

When you finish creating your Web page, you can use the Web Publishing Wizard to transfer the page to a Web server. Once the Web page is stored on the server, your page will be available to everyone on the Web.

If the Web Publishing Wizard is not available, you need to add the Web Publishing Wizard component from the Internet Tools category. To add a Windows component, see page 94.

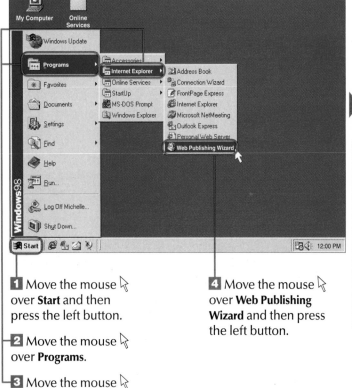

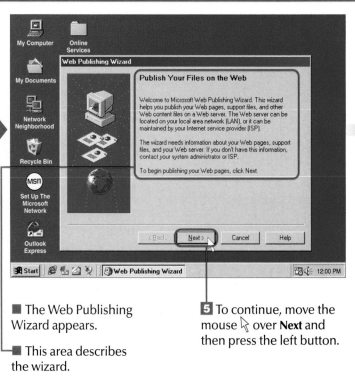

1 Move the mouse over **Start** and then press the left button.

2 Move the mouse over **Programs**.

3 Move the mouse over **Internet Explorer**.

4 Move the mouse over **Web Publishing Wizard** and then press the left button.

■ The Web Publishing Wizard appears.

■ This area describes the wizard.

5 To continue, move the mouse over **Next** and then press the left button.

Where can I publish my Web page?

The company that gives you access to the Internet usually offers space on its Web server where you can publish your Web page. There are also places on the Internet that will publish your Web page for free, such as GeoCities (www.geocities.com).

You can also publish your Web page on a corporate intranet. An intranet is a small version of the Internet within a company or organization. Ask your system administrator for details.

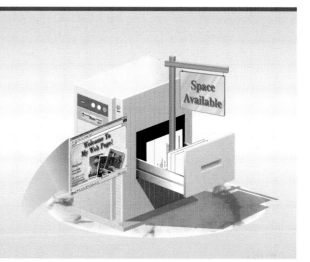

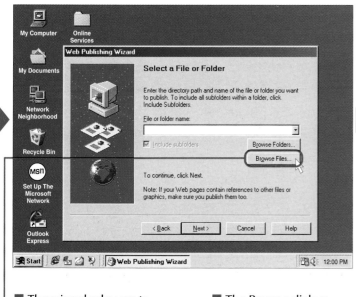

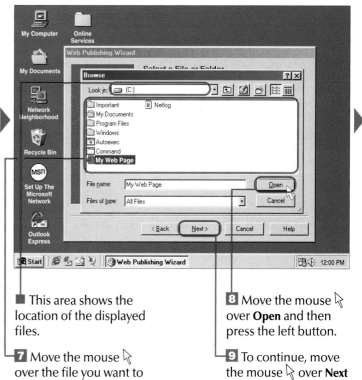

■ The wizard asks you to enter the name of the file you want to publish.

6 To locate the file you want to publish, move the mouse ⊷ over **Browse Files** and then press the left button.

■ The Browse dialog box appears.

■ This area shows the location of the displayed files.

7 Move the mouse ⊷ over the file you want to publish and then press the left button.

8 Move the mouse ⊷ over **Open** and then press the left button.

9 To continue, move the mouse ⊷ over **Next** and then press the left button.

CONTINUED➡

215

You need to enter information about your Web server to publish your Web page. If you do not have this information, ask your Internet service provider or system administrator.

You must know the following information to publish your Web page:

- Address you use to access your personal Web pages
- User name
- Password

PUBLISH WEB PAGES (CONTINUED)

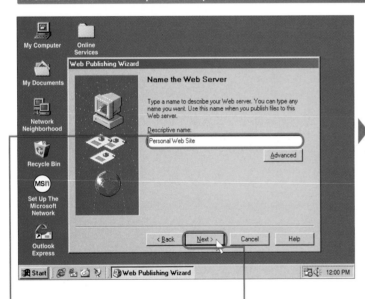

10 Type a name to describe your Web server.

Note: If you have published Web pages before, the wizard fills in the name of the Web server for you.

11 To continue, move the mouse ⌖ over **Next** and then press the left button.

12 Type the address you use to access your personal Web pages.

Note: If you have published Web pages before, this dialog box does not appear.

13 To continue, move the mouse ⌖ over **Next** and then press the left button.

If my Web page contains images, do I also need to publish the images?

If your Web page contains images or a background image, you also need to publish these files. If you do not publish the image files, an icon appears where the images should appear on the Web page.

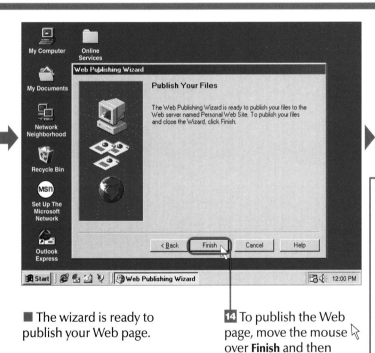

■ The wizard is ready to publish your Web page.

14 To publish the Web page, move the mouse ⃗ over **Finish** and then press the left button.

15 Type your user name and then press the **Tab** key.

16 Type your password.

Note: You will not have to enter the password the next time you publish Web pages.

17 Move the mouse ⃗ over **OK** and then press the left button.

■ A confirmation dialog box appears. To close the dialog box, move the mouse ⃗ over **OK** and then press the left button.

INDEX

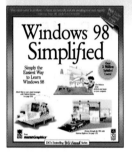
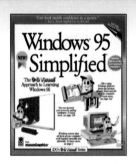

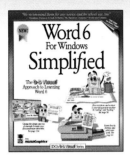

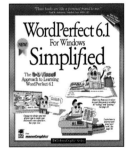

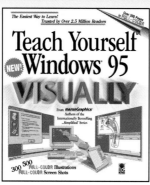

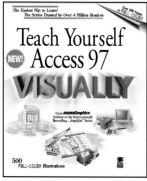

ORDER FORM

IDG BOOKS ®

TRADE & INDIVIDUAL ORDERS
Phone: **(800) 762-2974**
or **(317) 596-5200**
(8 a.m.–6 p.m., CST, weekdays)
FAX : **(800) 550-2747**
or **(317) 596-5692**

EDUCATIONAL ORDERS & DISCOUNTS
Phone: **(800) 434-2086**
(8:30 a.m.–5:00 p.m., CST, weekdays)
FAX : **(317) 596-5499**

CORPORATE ORDERS FOR 3-D VISUAL™ SERIES
Phone: **(800) 469-6616**
(8 a.m.–5 p.m., EST, weekdays)
FAX : **(905) 890-9434**

Qty	ISBN	Title	Price	Total

Shipping & Handling Charges

	Description	First book	Each add'l. book	Total
Domestic	Normal	$4.50	$1.50	$
	Two Day Air	$8.50	$2.50	$
	Overnight	$18.00	$3.00	$
International	Surface	$8.00	$8.00	$
	Airmail	$16.00	$16.00	$
	DHL Air	$17.00	$17.00	$

Subtotal _____

CA residents add applicable sales tax _____

IN, MA and MD residents add 5% sales tax _____

IL residents add 6.25% sales tax _____

RI residents add 7% sales tax _____

TX residents add 8.25% sales tax _____

Shipping _____

Total _____

Ship to:

Name_____

Address_____

Company_____

City/State/Zip_____

Daytime Phone_____

Payment: ☐ Check to IDG Books (US Funds Only)
☐ Visa ☐ Mastercard ☐ American Express

Card # _____ Exp. _____ Signature_____

***maranGraphics*™**